AF488539

JAGAT SANDHU

HALF ME HALF THE WORLD

Table of Contents

INTRODUCTION 9

Chapter 1: The Inner World 12

Chapter 2: The Outer World 15

Chapter 3: The Journey of Self-Discovery 19

Chapter 4: The Power of Connection 23

Chapter 5: Finding Strength in Adversity 25

Chapter 5: Finding Strength in Adversity 29

Chapter 7: The Voice Within – Listening to Yourself 33

Chapter 8: Learning from Others Without Losing Yourself 37

Chapter 9: Faith, Doubt, and the Search for Meaning 41

Chapter 10: Pain as a Teacher 45

Chapter 11: The Power of Silence and Stillness 50

Chapter 12: Love and Letting Go 55

Chapter 13: Purpose and the Quiet Voice Inside You 60

Chapter 13: Purpose and the Quiet Voice Inside You 65

Chapter 14: Pain, Struggle, and the Beauty of Endurance 70

Chapter 15: The Art of Stillness and the Power of the Present
Moment 74

Chapter 16: Voices of the World — What We Learn From Others 78

Chapter 17: Love, Loss, and the Lessons in Between 82

Chapter 18: Courage and Fear — The Dance of Life............................87

Chapter 19 : The Quiet Victories 92

Chapter 20: Becoming Your Own Home 97

Chapter 21: Finding Peace in a Chaotic World 102

Chapter 22: Trusting Yourself When No One Else Does 107

Chapter 23: The Power of Second Chances 112

Chapter 24: The People Who Leave and the Lessons They Leave
Behind 116

Chapter 25: Us — The Power of Connection 120

Chapter 26: The Mountain Is You 124

Chapter 27: When It Hurts, Write 128

Chapter 28: Those Who Stayed 133

Chapter 29: The Weight of Expectations...137

Chapter 30: The Power of Gratitude..143

Chapter 31: The Art of Saying No 148

Chapter 32: The Courage to Be Vulnerable 154

Chapter 33: The Healing Power of Nature.......................................159

Chapter 34: The Gift of Forgiveness 164

Chapter 35: The Strength in Asking for Help 169

Chapter 36: The Beauty of Imperfection 174

Chapter 37: The Power of Small Wins 179

Chapter 38: The Gift of Curiosity 184

Chapter 39: The Strength of Stillness 188

Chapter 40: The Power of Connection 193

Chapter 41: The Courage to Dream Big 198

Chapter 42: The Healing Power of Creativity 203

Chapter 43: The Strength of Resilience 208

Chapter 44: The Power of Presence 213

Chapter 45: The Gift of Self-Love 218

Chapter 46: The Power of Letting Go 223

Chapter 47: The Strength of Hope 228

Chapter 48: The Power of Authenticity 233

Chapter 49: The Power of Joy 238

Chapter 50: The Strength of Boundaries 241

Chapter 51: The Power of Forgiveness 246

Chapter 52: The Strength of Patience 251

Chapter 53: The Power of Community 256

Chapter 54: The Power of Purpose 261

Chapter 55: The Strength of Gratitude 266

Chapter 56: The Strength of Vulnerability 271

Chapter 57: The Power of Simplicity 276

Chapter 58: The Strength of Faith 281

Chapter 59: The Strength of Love 285

Chapter 60: The Journey Forward 289

Acknowledgments 294

INTRODUCTION

We all live two kinds of lives—one that happens inside us, and another that happens outside, in the world. This book, Half Me, Half the World, is about that balance. It is about the "me"—my feelings, thoughts, dreams, fears—and the "world"—people, relationships, challenges, and society. Both sides shape who we are.

This book is not a novel or a textbook. It's more like a mirror and a guide. In these pages, you'll find:

- Powerful quotes that make you stop and think.
- Stories of great people who faced hard times, stayed strong, and made a difference.
- Short stories that touch on love, pain, hope, truth, and the small moments that teach big lessons.

- Why This Book Matters

We often look outside for answers—to people, money, success, or approval. But sometimes, the real answers are inside us. Other times, the world around us teaches us lessons we never expected. This book brings both together.

You might ask:

- What is my purpose?
- Why do I feel lost, even when I have everything?
- Why do some people change the world, while others stay stuck?

This book doesn't give direct answers. Instead, it offers examples, experiences, and inspirations to help you find your own answers.

What You'll Find in This Book

- You'll see how religion, in its true spirit, gives us comfort and courage during hard times.
- You'll explore the deep, emotional world of writers like Fyodor Dostoevsky, who showed us the light inside the darkness.

- You'll come across short stories—some true, some imagined—that reflect the same emotions we all feel but often can't express.

Each chapter, each quote, each story is like a step on a journey—the journey to understand yourself and your place in the world.

The Meaning of the Title: Half Me, Half the World

The title says it all.

We are not just what we think or feel—we are also shaped by what we see, whom we meet, and how we respond to the world. This book is about keeping both sides alive:

- "Half Me" is your inner world—your soul, emotions, fears, and dreams.
- "Half the World" is the people, events, and challenges that shape you from the outside.

When you learn to listen to both sides, you find peace, purpose, and power.

A Message from the Author

I am not a preacher or a philosopher. I am a human being—just like you—trying to understand life. These are the thoughts, stories, and lessons that have touched me deeply. I've put them together in this book with honesty and heart.

If even one page brings you clarity, comfort, or courage—then this book has done its job.　＿＿ Jagat Sandhu

Chapter 1: The Inner World

What is the Inner Me?

Inside each of us, there is a special world—a world of our thoughts, feelings, and dreams. This inner world is like a garden that we carry with us every day. Some days, the garden feels beautiful, filled with bright flowers like happiness, hope, and peace. Other days, it might feel a little messy, with weeds like anger, sadness, or fear. But just like a real garden, the more we care for it, the better it can grow.

When we feel good inside, like when we're calm or proud of ourselves, it's like our garden is full of colorful flowers. But when we're upset, worried, or afraid, the garden can feel full of weeds. The good news is, we have the power to take care of our inner world. And just like any garden, it takes practice and attention.

Taking Care of Your Inner Garden

Just like how a garden needs water, sunlight, and care to grow, our inner world needs certain things too. When we feel upset, it's important to stop and figure out why we feel that way. Maybe we're worried about something happening in our life, or maybe we're just feeling tired and need some rest.

Sometimes, we don't even realize that we're upset. We might be carrying a lot of stress without knowing it. That's why taking time to listen to how we feel is so important. It's like checking the plants in your garden to see if they need more water or sunlight.

How can we take care of our inner garden? The first step is to be kind to ourselves. If you make a mistake, don't be too hard on yourself. Everyone makes mistakes. Instead of being upset with yourself, try to learn from it and grow. If you're feeling sad, it's okay. It's normal to feel sad sometimes. The important thing is to not let that sadness stay too long.

You can also talk to yourself kindly. If a friend was feeling sad, you wouldn't tell them, "You should never be sad!" Instead, you'd say, "It's okay to feel sad. What can I do to help you feel better?" So, when you feel bad, try talking to yourself in a gentle way, like you would talk to a friend.

The Power of Self-Reflection

One way to take care of your inner world is by taking time to reflect. Reflection means looking back at what's happened, thinking about how you felt, and learning from it. For example, after a hard day, ask yourself, "How did I feel today?" "What made me happy?" "What made me upset?" Taking a few minutes each day to think about your feelings can help you understand yourself better.

You don't have to do this all the time, but every now and then, try to sit quietly and think about your day. What went well? What could you do better next time? This helps you grow and become stronger.

"The most important thing is to enjoy your life—to be happy—it's all that matters."

— Audrey Hepburn

Audrey Hepburn's quote is a simple but powerful reminder. No matter what happens around us, the most important thing is to be happy. Happiness doesn't come from having the most toys or the nicest clothes. It comes from feeling good inside, from loving who you are and being content with your life.

Dealing with Inner Conflicts

Sometimes, we feel torn between two choices. Maybe you want to go play outside, but you also need to finish your homework. This is called inner conflict—a battle inside your heart. It's normal to feel this way. We all have times when we can't decide what to do.

The best way to handle this is to listen to your feelings. Ask yourself: What will make me feel good in the long run? Will finishing your homework help you feel proud of yourself? Or will playing outside make you feel happy and relaxed? Sometimes, you have to balance both. You can do a little homework and then go outside to play, giving yourself both rest and achievement.

Inner conflicts don't have to be scary. They just mean you're thinking carefully about your choices. When you listen to your heart and mind, the right decision becomes clearer.

Chapter 2: The Outer World

The People Around Us

Now let's talk about the world outside of you. This is your outer world, and it includes the people you meet, the experiences you have, and the things that happen around you. Think of it like a big playground full of different games, friends, and challenges. The people in this playground can make you feel happy, sad, excited, or angry.

Some people, like your family or good friends, help you feel loved and supported. They encourage you when you need it and help you when you're feeling down. But there are also people who might make you feel bad about yourself. Maybe they tease you or say unkind things. When this happens, it's important to remember that you can choose who you spend time with.

The people who make you feel good and help you grow are the ones you want to spend more time with. They lift you up and make you feel strong. If you are around people who are always negative or make you feel bad, it can bring you down too. That's why it's important to choose friends who treat you kindly.

"You are the average of the five people you spend the most time with."

— Jim Rohn

This quote means that the people you spend time with can change how you feel and think. If you're always around people who are positive and kind, you'll start to feel the same way. But if you spend too much time with people who are negative or hurtful, it can bring you down.

Think about your friends. Do they make you feel happy and strong? Or do they make you feel sad and tired? Choose to be around people who bring out the best in you.

How the World Teaches Us Lessons

The outer world is full of lessons—sometimes through difficult things that happen. Life isn't always easy. We all face problems, big and small. Maybe you fail a test, or maybe something doesn't go the way you planned. But even these hard moments can teach you important lessons.

When something goes wrong, instead of feeling upset, ask yourself, "What can I learn from this?" Maybe you learned that you need to study harder next time, or maybe you learned that it's okay to ask for help when you need it. The world around us is always teaching us something. Every challenge can help us grow and become better.

The Fisherman and the Businessman

Here's a simple story to help you understand that everyone has different ideas of what success means.

A businessman walked along the beach and saw a fisherman relaxing. The businessman asked him, "Why aren't you working harder? You could catch more fish, make more money, and have a better life."

The fisherman smiled and said, "I already catch enough fish to feed my family. I enjoy my life, and I'm happy."

The businessman thought for a moment and said, "But if you worked harder, you could get richer, hire more people, and enjoy life even more!"

The fisherman thought for a second and replied, "But that's exactly what I'm doing now. I enjoy my life as it is."

This story shows us that everyone has different ideas of success. For the businessman, success meant having lots of money and a big company. But for the fisherman, success meant being happy with what he had. You don't always need everything the world tells you to want. What makes you happy might be different, and that's okay.

Finding Balance Between the Inner and Outer Worlds

Now that we've talked about both the inner world (your feelings) and the outer world (the people and things around you), the key to living a happy life is balance. You can't only focus on how you feel inside or just worry about what's happening outside of you. Both are important.

When you take care of your inner world—by being kind to yourself, thinking positively, and listening to your feelings—you'll be able to deal with challenges better. And when you surround yourself with positive people and learn from the world around you, you grow and feel stronger.

Take a moment and think about these questions:

• How are you feeling today? Are you happy, sad, or something else?

• Who are the people around you? Are they making you feel good or bad?

• What lessons have you learned recently? What can you do better next time?

Remember, the goal is balance. Taking care of your inner world and your outer world is the key to living a happy and peaceful life.

Chapter 3: The Journey of Self-Discovery

What is Self-Discovery?

Self-discovery is like opening a treasure chest inside yourself. At first, the chest might seem closed, locked up by fears and doubts. But as you begin the journey of looking inside yourself, you'll find pieces of gold—your strengths, your passions, and your true potential.

Sometimes, you may feel lost. You may wonder, "Who am I really?" or "What's my purpose in life?" That's perfectly normal. In fact, every person, at some point in their life, wonders about these questions. The truth is, self-discovery is a lifelong journey. It's not about finding one big answer—it's about understanding yourself bit by bit.

: The Lost Key

Imagine a young boy named Sam. Sam always followed what everyone else told him to do. He wore the clothes his friends wore, played the games they played, and even tried to like the same things they liked. But deep down, Sam felt empty. He thought, "Why do I feel so different inside? Everyone else seems so sure of themselves."

One day, Sam's grandmother gave him a beautiful old key. She told him, "This key will unlock the door to your true self. But you must go on a journey to find it."

Sam didn't understand what she meant, but he decided to go on an adventure. He tried new hobbies, spent time alone in nature, and even talked to new people. Along the way, he discovered things about himself—things he loved, things he feared, and things that made him excited.

At the end of his journey, Sam didn't find the key hidden in a box. Instead, he realized that he was the key. The more he explored his thoughts, feelings, and dreams, the closer he got to understanding who he really was.

This story shows that self-discovery doesn't happen in a day. It takes time, and it often requires you to try new things, face your fears, and step outside your comfort zone.

The Power of Change

Change can be scary. Maybe you've experienced a change that was difficult—a new school, a move to a different city, or a change in your family. These moments often feel overwhelming because we're used to things staying the same. But change is a powerful force, and it can bring about amazing growth.

When you step into the unknown, you often learn more about yourself than you would if everything stayed the same. It's like planting a tree in new soil. At first, it might not feel comfortable. But with time, the roots grow deeper, and the tree becomes stronger.

One of the most powerful lessons in life is to embrace change. Don't run from it. Sometimes, the most beautiful flowers grow from the most unexpected places.

"Life is 10% what happens to us and 90% how we react to it."

— Charles R. Swindoll

This quote reminds us that life will always bring challenges and changes. We can't control everything that happens around us, but we can control how we react. If we choose to face change with an open heart and a positive attitude, we can grow from it, no matter how hard it seems at first.

The Art of Letting Go

One of the hardest things to do in life is to let go. Whether it's letting go of a dream, a friendship, or an old way of thinking, it's not easy. But sometimes, letting go is the only way to move forward.

Imagine carrying a heavy backpack filled with old rocks. Every time you try to walk, the backpack weighs you down. It might be filled with memories, regrets, or fears. The longer you carry it, the harder it becomes to walk.

But what if you decided to let go of some of those rocks? What if you put them down, one by one, and walked a little lighter?

Letting go doesn't mean forgetting or ignoring your past. It means understanding that your past doesn't have to control your future. You are not your mistakes, and you are not your fears. You are the person you choose to be right now, and that person can always grow.

: The Burden of the Past

There was once a man who carried the burden of past mistakes for many years. He couldn't forgive himself for hurting his friends, or for missing important moments in his life. He thought about these mistakes every day, and they weighed him down.

One day, he met a wise woman who asked, "Why are you carrying all this heavy baggage? Why are you letting your past steal your present joy?"

He thought for a moment and realized she was right. He had been carrying those old mistakes for so long that he forgot how to move forward.

The wise woman told him, "You can't change the past, but you can choose to forgive yourself. Let go of the weight you carry, and you'll feel lighter."

That was the turning point for the man. Slowly but surely, he started to let go of the guilt and regret. As he did, he began to feel freer, and his life became brighter.

Chapter 4: The Power of Connection

Building Meaningful Relationships

The people around us have a huge impact on our lives. Think about the people who make you feel happy, supported, and loved. These are the people who lift you up when you're down. They're like the sun in your life's sky, warming you with their kindness and light.

But not all relationships are like this. Sometimes, we're surrounded by people who make us feel bad about ourselves. Maybe they're rude, negative, or even make us feel smaller. It's important to remember that you don't have to keep those people in your life. You can choose the people who make you feel good and let go of the ones who hold you back.

The Gift of Listening

One of the best gifts we can give someone is our full attention. When you really listen to someone—without thinking about your own problems or checking your phone—you are giving them something precious: your time, your focus, and your care.

In our busy world, it's easy to forget how powerful listening can be. But just imagine what it would be like if someone listened to you like that. How would it make you feel?

Listening isn't just about hearing words. It's about understanding the feelings behind those words. It's about being there for someone when they need you the most.

"The most precious gift we can offer anyone is our attention."

— ThichNhatHanh

This simple quote is a reminder that true connection happens when we listen. The next time someone shares something with you, give them your full attention. You'll be amazed at how much deeper your relationships can become.

The Power of Small Acts of Kindness

Small acts of kindness—like holding the door open for someone, offering a compliment, or simply saying "thank you"—can make a big difference. These small gestures might seem insignificant, but they have the power to change someone's day.

One of the most beautiful things about kindness is that it's free. You don't need money to be kind. A kind word, a smile, or a helping hand can create ripples of goodness in the world.

Think about your relationships. Are there people in your life who make you feel good and help you grow? How can you be a better listener? How can you spread kindness in your own life?

This new section keeps the reader engaged by offering valuable life lessons, stories that are easy to connect with, and prompts for reflection. The stories, quotes, and examples build on the theme of the book and encourage the reader to think deeply about their own journey of self-discovery, change, and connection.

Chapter 5: Finding Strength in Adversity

Why Tough Times Matter

Adversity. Challenges. Difficulties. These are words we all know too well. But what if I told you that the hardest moments in life could actually become the most important ones?

When life is easy, we don't grow much. We stay comfortable in our little bubbles. But when things get tough, that's when we learn who we really are. It's like a seed that needs to break through the hard ground before it can grow into a beautiful tree. The struggle is what makes the tree strong.

The Power of Persistence

Imagine you're walking through a forest, and there's a giant boulder in your way. At first, you try to push it, but it doesn't move. You think about giving up. But then you remember something: sometimes, it's not about moving the boulder right away. It's about trying again and again, even when it seems impossible.

Persistence is what keeps us going when things don't work out the first time. It's about believing that even small steps forward can lead to big changes.

"The greatest glory in living lies not in never falling, but in rising every time we fall."

— Nelson Mandela

Mandela's words remind us that falling doesn't mean failure. It means we're trying, learning, and growing. Every time we pick ourselves up, we become a little stronger, a little braver.

: Overcoming Fear

There was once a young girl named Lila. She was afraid of speaking in front of people. Whenever she had to give a speech at school, her heart would race, her hands would shake, and her mind would go blank. She thought she'd never be able to do it.

But Lila didn't give up. She practiced every day, standing in front of her mirror, talking to herself as if she were giving a speech. It felt strange at first, but little by little, she grew more confident.

The day of her big speech arrived, and Lila was nervous, but she remembered all her practice. She stood tall, took a deep breath, and spoke from her heart. And guess what? She did great. She didn't let her fear stop her. She used it as fuel to keep going.

Lila's story shows us that sometimes, the things we're most afraid of are the very things that help us grow. When you face your fears, you realize that you're capable of so much more than you thought.

The Role of Pain in Growth

Pain is often seen as something negative, something we want to avoid at all costs. But pain, both emotional and physical, is a teacher. It forces us to stop and think. It asks us to reflect on where we are and where we want to go.

Pain can show us our weaknesses, but it can also show us our strength. When we experience pain, we learn how to cope, how to heal, and how to rise above it. Without pain, we might never know what we're capable of.

One famous example is the life of Oprah Winfrey. Before becoming the media mogul we all know today, Oprah faced immense challenges. She grew up in poverty, faced rejection, and endured painful experiences. Yet, instead of giving up, she used those painful moments as fuel for her success. Oprah turned her struggles into a message of hope for others.

"Where there is no struggle, there is no strength."

— Oprah Winfrey

Oprah's story reminds us that every struggle is an opportunity for growth. It's in the toughest moments that we discover just how strong we really are.

Resilience: Bouncing Back from Setbacks

Resilience is the ability to bounce back from difficult situations. It's not about avoiding problems but facing them with the strength to overcome them. Life will always bring challenges, but resilience allows us to keep going, no matter what.

Take the example of J.K. Rowling, the author of the Harry Potter series. Before her books became a global phenomenon, Rowling faced many rejections from publishers. She was living as a single mother, struggling to make ends meet. But she didn't give up on her dream. Instead of listening to the rejections, she kept writing. Her resilience paid off when the first book in the Harry Potter series was finally published.

Her story teaches us that setbacks don't define us. How we respond to them does.

"It is not the strongest of the species that survive, nor the most intelligent, but the one most responsive to change."

— Charles Darwin

Darwin's words remind us that it's not about being the smartest or the strongest. It's about how we respond to the challenges life throws at us. The more adaptable and resilient we are, the more likely we are to succeed.

Chapter 5: Finding Strength in Adversity

Why Tough Times Matter

Adversity. Challenges. Difficulties. These are words we all know too well. But what if I told you that the hardest moments in life could actually become the most important ones?

When life is easy, we don't grow much. We stay comfortable in our little bubbles. But when things get tough, that's when we learn who we really are. It's like a seed that needs to break through the hard ground before it can grow into a beautiful tree. The struggle is what makes the tree strong.

The Power of Persistence

Imagine you're walking through a forest, and there's a giant boulder in your way. At first, you try to push it, but it doesn't move. You think about giving up. But then you remember something: sometimes, it's not about moving the boulder right away. It's about trying again and again, even when it seems impossible.

Persistence is what keeps us going when things don't work out the first time. It's about believing that even small steps forward can lead to big changes.

"The greatest glory in living lies not in never falling, but in rising every time we fall."

— Nelson Mandela

Mandela's words remind us that falling doesn't mean failure. It means we're trying, learning, and growing. Every time we pick ourselves up, we become a little stronger, a little braver.

: Overcoming Fear

There was once a young girl named Lila. She was afraid of speaking in front of people. Whenever she had to give a speech at school, her heart would race, her hands would shake, and her mind would go blank. She thought she'd never be able to do it.

But Lila didn't give up. She practiced every day, standing in front of her mirror, talking to herself as if she were giving a speech. It felt strange at first, but little by little, she grew more confident.

The day of her big speech arrived, and Lila was nervous, but she remembered all her practice. She stood tall, took a deep breath, and spoke from her heart. And guess what? She did great. She didn't let her fear stop her. She used it as fuel to keep going.

Lila's story shows us that sometimes, the things we're most afraid of are the very things that help us grow. When you face your fears, you realize that you're capable of so much more than you thought.

The Role of Pain in Growth

Pain is often seen as something negative, something we want to avoid at all costs. But pain, both emotional and physical, is a teacher. It forces us to stop and think. It asks us to reflect on where we are and where we want to go.

Pain can show us our weaknesses, but it can also show us our strength. When we experience pain, we learn how to cope, how to heal, and how to rise above it. Without pain, we might never know what we're capable of.

One famous example is the life of Oprah Winfrey. Before becoming the media mogul we all know today, Oprah faced immense challenges. She grew up in poverty, faced rejection, and endured painful experiences. Yet, instead of giving up, she used those painful moments as fuel for her success. Oprah turned her struggles into a message of hope for others.

"Where there is no struggle, there is no strength."

— Oprah Winfrey

Oprah's story reminds us that every struggle is an opportunity for growth. It's in the toughest moments that we discover just how strong we really are.

Resilience: Bouncing Back from Setbacks

Resilience is the ability to bounce back from difficult situations. It's not about avoiding problems but facing them with the strength to overcome them. Life will always bring challenges, but resilience allows us to keep going, no matter what.

Take the example of J.K. Rowling, the author of the Harry Potter series. Before her books became a global phenomenon, Rowling faced many rejections from publishers. She was living as a single mother, struggling to make ends meet. But she didn't give up on her dream. Instead of listening to the rejections, she kept writing. Her resilience paid off when the first book in the Harry Potter series was finally published.

Her story teaches us that setbacks don't define us. How we respond to them does.

"It is not the strongest of the species that survive, nor the most intelligent, but the one most responsive to change."

— Charles Darwin

Darwin's words remind us that it's not about being the smartest or the strongest. It's about how we respond to the challenges life throws at us. The more adaptable and resilient we are, the more likely we are to succeed.

Chapter 7: The Voice Within – Listening to Yourself

What Is the Inner Voice?

Have you ever felt something deep inside telling you what's right or wrong—even when the world around you is saying something else? That quiet feeling, that little voice inside, is your inner voice. It's not loud. It doesn't shout. But if you pay attention, it always guides you in the right direction.

This voice is your heart, your conscience, your soul. And listening to it is one of the most important things you can learn to do in life.

Why Do We Ignore It?

In today's noisy world, we are often surrounded by the opinions of others—social media, friends, family, and even strangers. Everyone has something to say. We get so used to listening to others that we forget to listen to ourselves.

Sometimes, we already know what we want or what's right for us, but we doubt ourselves. We don't trust our gut. Why? Because we're afraid of being wrong, or we want to please others. But the truth is—when you ignore your own voice for too long, you lose your way.

"When you listen to your own voice, you find your true path."

— From Half Me, Half the World

: The Boy and the Painting

Once, there was a boy who loved painting. He would spend hours mixing colors and drawing scenes from his imagination. But his parents wanted him to become a doctor. They told him painting was just a hobby, not a career. So, the boy stopped painting.

Years passed. He studied hard, became a doctor, and made good money. But something always felt missing. One day, he found his old paintbrushes in a box. He held them and smiled, tears in his eyes. It was like his inner child was calling out, saying, "You never stopped loving this."

That day, he started painting again. And though he still worked as a doctor, he felt more complete—because he finally listened to his inner voice.

What Religion Teaches Us About the Inner Voice

All major religions talk about the importance of inner truth—that God or the Divine often speaks through silence, through our heart.

"One must lift oneself by one's own mind, not degrade oneself. The mind is the friend of the conditioned soul, and also its enemy."

— Bhagavad Gita, Chapter 6, Shloka 5

This shloka teaches that our own mind can either help us rise or bring us down. The choice depends on whether we listen to the good, wise part of ourselves.

"Man jeete jag jeet."

("Conquer your mind, and you will conquer the world.")

This line teaches us that all power starts inside us. If we can understand and control our own thoughts and emotions, no outside situation can defeat us.

"The kingdom of God is within you."

— Luke 17:21

This means we don't have to go far to find peace or God. We just have to look within. The answers are already inside us.

Simple Practice: Listening to Yourself

Here's a small exercise to help you reconnect with your inner voice:

1.   Sit quietly for 5 minutes. Turn off your phone. Close your eyes.

2.   Breathe deeply. Don't try to think. Just listen.

3.   Ask yourself:

- What am I feeling right now?

- What do I really want?

- What's something I've been avoiding?

Write down whatever comes to you—no judgment. Just be honest.

"The mind is a superb instrument if used rightly. Used wrongly, however, it becomes very destructive."

This reminds us that being aware of our thoughts helps us separate the noise from the truth.

Closing Thoughts:

Your inner voice is like a compass. It won't always give you loud, clear directions, but it will gently show you the way—if you're willing to listen. When you follow that voice, you walk a path that's truly your own.

And remember: Your truth doesn't need to be loud to be real. It just needs to be yours.

Chapter 8: Learning from Others Without Losing Yourself

We Learn by Watching Others

From childhood, we learn by looking at the world around us. We copy our parents, teachers, friends—even strangers. This is natural. It helps us understand how life works. But as we grow, something important happens: we must learn to choose what to follow and what to leave behind.

Not everything we see or hear is right for us. And not every path is your path.

Learning from others is good—but losing yourself in the process is not.

The Imitation Trap

Have you ever seen someone doing well and thought, "Maybe I should do that too"?

Maybe your friend is successful in business, so you start thinking business is your dream too. But deep down, your heart might belong to writing, teaching, or helping people.

Trying to follow someone else's dream can leave you feeling empty—even if you "succeed." Why? Because it was never truly your dream.

"Be yourself. Everyone else is already taken."

— Oscar Wilde

This quote is simple but powerful. You are one of a kind. The world doesn't need another copy—it needs the original you.

: The Story of Elon Musk and Dr. A.P.J. Abdul Kalam

Elon Musk and Dr. Kalam were both brilliant minds who dreamed big. But their dreams were completely different.

•	Elon Musk wanted to take humanity to Mars. His focus was on space, innovation, and risk-taking in business.

•	Dr. Kalam, on the other hand, focused on peace, education, and simple living. He stayed humble, always working for others.

If Kalam had tried to become like Musk—or Musk like Kalam—they would not have changed the world in the way they did. They stayed true to their path, and that's why they succeeded.

Religion Says: Be True to Your Nature

"It is better to live your own destiny imperfectly than to live an imitation of somebody else's life with perfection."

— Gita Chapter 3, Verse 35

This shloka tells us that even if we make mistakes while following our own path, it's still better than copying others.

"Aapanhathhiaapnaaape he kaajsavaariye."

("With our own hands, we shape our own lives.")

No one else can walk your journey. You have to walk it yourself, with courage and honesty.

Learning vs. Imitating

There's a difference between learning from someone and imitating them.

- Learning is when you take the wisdom and apply it in your own way.

- Imitating is when you copy without thinking if it fits you.

For example, reading about Stoicism can teach you how to stay calm. But it doesn't mean you have to become a Stoic monk. Instead, you take what works—like controlling your emotions—and leave the rest.

"You don't control what happens, but you can control how you respond."

This is a lesson you can apply in your own way. You don't have to live like Marcus Aurelius to be wise.

: The Mirror and the Window

There was a man who spent his whole life trying to become like his mentor. He dressed like him, talked like him, and even tried to think like him. But he never felt happy.

One day, a child asked him, "Why do you always look at others like they are the answer? Why don't you look in the mirror and see who you are?"

The man realized something powerful. He had been looking through windows at others instead of looking in the mirror to find himself.

Take the Best, Leave the Rest

Look at life like a giant buffet. You don't have to eat everything. You take what suits your taste, your health, your hunger. Learning from the world is the same. Pick the values, ideas, and lessons that fit your soul.

Be open to learning—but be rooted in yourself.

Your Unique Map

Take a blank page. Write down:

- 3 people you admire

- What you admire about them

- How you can apply those things in your own way

This helps you stay inspired but not lost. It helps you stay you.

You are not here to become someone else.

You are here to become the best version of yourself.

So learn, grow, and evolve—but never lose your own voice in the crowd.

Chapter 9: Faith, Doubt, and the Search for Meaning

What Is Faith?

Faith is like a quiet strength. It's believing in something—even when you can't see it. It could be belief in God, in love, in a better future, or even in yourself.

Faith doesn't always have to be religious. Sometimes, it's as simple as trusting that the sun will rise again after a dark night. That things will get better, even when they feel broken. That you'll heal, even when you're hurting.

But alongside faith, there is something else: doubt. And that's okay too.

Faith and Doubt Can Live Together

People think faith and doubt are enemies—but they're not. Doubt makes your faith stronger. When you question, explore, and feel unsure, you grow. You go deeper.

Imagine climbing a mountain. Faith is what keeps you going, but doubt is what makes you check your steps carefully. Without both, you may fall.

"Doubt isn't the opposite of faith; it's part of it."

— From Half Me, Half the World

Story The Candle in the Cave

Once, a traveler got lost in a dark cave. He had only one small candle. The flame was weak. He thought, "This won't be enough." But he walked with it anyway. Step by step, the tiny light helped him find his way out.

That candle is like faith—small, sometimes shaky, but still enough to guide you through darkness.

From the Holy Books

Quran:

"So truly where there is hardship, there is also ease."

— SurahAsh-Sharh 94:6

This reminds us that no matter how deep our struggle is, relief will come. Faith helps us wait for that moment.

Bible:

"Faith is the substance of things hoped for, the evidence of things not seen."

— Hebrews 11:1

You don't always need proof to believe. Sometimes, belief itself is enough to keep you moving.

Bhagavad Gita:

"One who has faith, who is devoted and has control over the senses, gains knowledge. And having gained knowledge, he quickly attains supreme peace."

— Chapter 4, Verse 39

Faith helps us find wisdom, and wisdom brings peace.

Guru Granth Sahib:

"Nanak says: He who has no faith, is forever in doubt, and wanders lost."

— Guru Nanak Dev Ji

This teaches us that faith is not just belief—it's the anchor that keeps us from drifting in life's storms.

When You Feel Lost

It's normal to feel confused. Everyone—yes, everyone—goes through moments when they ask:

- "What is the purpose of my life?"
- "Why is this happening to me?"
- "Is anyone listening up there?"

Even great minds like Fyodor Dostoevsky battled with faith and doubt. In his books like The Brothers Karamazov, he showed how people struggle to believe in goodness when there's so much pain in the world.

But even in that pain, there's beauty. That struggle makes us human.

"He who has a why to live can bear almost any how."

This means if you know why you are here, even the hardest days won't break you. Faith gives you that "why."

Faith Is Personal

Faith doesn't look the same for everyone. For one person, it may be going to the temple every day. For another, it might be helping someone in need. And for someone else, just getting out of bed during depression can be an act of faith.

Don't compare your faith. Don't measure it. Just live it.

Simple Practice: A Note to Your Future Self

Take a pen and write a letter to your future self. Begin with:

> "Dear future me, I don't know how things will turn out, but I believe you will find your way. I trust in your strength, in life's lessons, and in the quiet support that is always around…"

Keep this note. Read it when you feel lost.

Faith doesn't always roar. Sometimes, it whispers:

> "Just take one more step."

And sometimes, that's all you need.

So, when the world feels heavy, when doubt feels loud—close your eyes, breathe deep, and remember:

There is meaning in the mess. There is light in the dark. And there is faith in your heart.

Chapter 10: Pain as a Teacher

Pain Hurts, But It Also Heals

No one likes pain. It's uncomfortable. It makes us cry, question everything, and sometimes feel like giving up. But pain, when we look at it closely, is also a teacher. It shows us what matters. It wakes us up. It helps us grow.

Just like a seed breaks open in darkness before it becomes a tree, we, too, grow stronger after pain.

"Out of suffering have emerged the strongest souls; the most massive characters are seared with scars."

— Khalil Gibran

Scars are not signs of weakness. They are signs of survival.

Pain Can Come in Many Forms

- The pain of losing someone you love

- The pain of failure

- The pain of being misunderstood

- The pain of feeling alone

But behind each of these is a message—something to learn.

From The Power of Now by EckhartTolle:

"The pain that you create now is always some form of nonacceptance, some form of unconscious resistance to what is."

Sometimes, we suffer more not because of what happened—but because we cannot accept it. Learning to accept pain is the first step to healing.

Religious Teachings on Pain

Guru Granth Sahib Ji:

"Dukhdaaroo sukh rogbhaiaa ja sukh taam na hoi."

("Pain is the medicine, and pleasure the disease; where there is pleasure, there is no desire for God.")

— Guru Nanak Dev Ji

This teaches us that pain brings us closer to truth, to ourselves, and to God. When everything is easy, we forget to look within.

Bible:

"Blessed are those who mourn, for they shall be comforted."

— Matthew 5:4

This shows us that even in sadness, comfort will come. God sees your tears.

Quran:

"Indeed, with hardship comes ease."

— SurahAsh-Sharh 94:6

This verse reminds us that pain is never permanent. Relief is always near.

Bhagavad Gita:

"A person who is not disturbed by sorrow and joy, who remains steady, becomes eligible for liberation."

— Chapter 2, Verse 15

When we stay calm in both happiness and pain, we become wise and free.

The Broken Pot

In a village, a woman carried water in two pots every day. One pot was perfect. The other had a crack and leaked water. The broken pot felt ashamed.

One day, the pot said, "I am useless."

The woman smiled and said, "Look behind you."

Along the path, beautiful flowers had grown—only on the side where the cracked pot dripped water.

"I planted seeds there," she said, "and your drops watered them every day."

Our pain may seem useless. But sometimes, it helps grow beauty we can't see yet.

From David Goggins' Life:

David Goggins is a former Navy SEAL who faced bullying, racism, and deep fear. Instead of running away, he turned pain into power.

He says:

"If you can get through doing things that you hate to do, on the other side is greatness."

Pain is part of the path. It doesn't block the way—it is the way.

What Pain Teaches Us

•	Empathy: When we hurt, we understand others better.

•	Strength: We find out how much we can truly handle.

•	Gratitude: After the pain, we learn to appreciate joy.

•	Purpose: Pain often leads us to a deeper reason for living.

: A Pain Journal

Write down a moment of pain from your life. Then write:

•	What did it teach me?

•	What did I become after it?

•	Who did it help me understand better?

This turns pain into a lesson—not just a memory.

Final Words of This Chapter

Pain changes people. But not always in a bad way.

It can break you—but it can also build you.

It can silence you—but also teach you to speak with more heart.

It can push you down—but also help you rise higher than ever before.

So when pain comes, don't run. Don't hide.

Sit with it. Learn from it. Then walk forward—wiser, softer, stronger.

Chapter 11: The Power of Silence and Stillness

In a Loud World, Silence is a Gift

The world is loud—phones buzzing, people talking, thoughts racing, social media never stopping. In this noise, we often forget what our own voice sounds like. That's why silence is so important.

Silence is not just the absence of sound.

It's the presence of awareness.

Stillness doesn't mean doing nothing.

It means being fully alive in this moment, without rushing to the next.

"Silence is not empty. It's full of answers."

— From Half Me, Half the World

Why Do We Fear Silence?

Many people feel uncomfortable in silence because they don't want to face their own thoughts. They keep busy, scroll endlessly, or talk without purpose—just to avoid stillness.

But here's a truth:

The answers we seek don't always come from outside.

They come when we slow down, sit with ourselves, and listen.

Religious Teachings on Silence

Guru Granth Sahib Ji:

"Chupaichup na hovaijelaa-erahaa liv taar."

("Silence alone doesn't bring peace unless one is truly connected to the Divine.")

Silence is not just closing your mouth. It is calming your soul and connecting deeply to truth.

Bible:

"Be still, and know that I am God."

— Psalm 46:10

Stillness opens the door to divine wisdom. In that quiet space, you feel God's presence.

Quran:

While the Quran does not directly speak of silence in isolation, the concept of "Tafakkur" (deep reflection) is highly encouraged:

"Do they not reflect within themselves?"

— Surah Ar-Rum 30:8

True reflection requires silence and presence.

Bhagavad Gita:

"A person who is silent, content with simple things, who controls the mind and body, and is devoted—such a person is dear to me."

— Chapter 12, Verse 16

Spiritual growth often happens in silence, not in noise.

Stillness in Modern Wisdom

EckhartTolle (The Power of Now):

"Stillness is where creativity and solutions to problems are found."

When you are fully present—not caught in thoughts about the past or worries about the future—you tap into a deeper intelligence.

Ryan Holiday (The Daily Stoic):

"All of humanity's problems stem from man's inability to sit quietly in a room alone."

— Borrowed from Blaise Pascal, often quoted in Stoic practice

True strength is not shouting. It's sitting still with peace.

SpThe Wise Monk's Silence

A young man once traveled to meet a wise monk known for his deep wisdom. When he arrived, the monk said nothing. They sat in silence.

After an hour, the young man asked, "Why don't you speak?"

The monk smiled and replied, "You came looking for wisdom. Wisdom speaks loudest in silence. Were you listening?"

How to Practice Stillness and Silence

1.   Start small: Just 5 minutes a day with no phone, no talking, no distractions.

2.   Breathe deeply: Focus only on your breath. Inhale peace, exhale noise.

3.   Observe your thoughts: Let them come and go like clouds. Don't judge them.

4.   Go for a silent walk: Leave your phone. Listen to nature, your footsteps, your heartbeat.

5.   Create a "quiet corner": A place in your room where you go to be with yourself.

Osho (The Book of Man):

"In silence, you meet your real self for the first time."

Osho believed that without silence, man lives a borrowed life—full of noise, but no depth.

Why Stillness Matters

- It helps you heal.

- It clears your mind.

- It reduces anxiety and overthinking.

- It allows new ideas to be born.

- It connects you to the world in a deeper way.

Sometimes, doing nothing is the most powerful thing you can do.

: One-Minute Reset

Close your eyes.

Breathe in deeply.

Hold for 4 seconds.

Breathe out slowly.

Repeat.

Do it anytime your world feels too loud.

Final Words of This Chapter

Silence is not loneliness.

Stillness is not laziness.

They are tools—sacred spaces—where you reconnect with yourself and the universe.

So the next time life feels noisy, remember:

The world may be loud, but your soul speaks softly.

Listen. It has much to say.

Chapter 12: Love and Letting Go

Love Teaches Us. Letting Go Frees Us.

Love is one of the deepest feelings a human can experience. It fills us with warmth, gives meaning to our days, and makes life feel beautiful. But love is not always easy. Sometimes, the people we love leave. Sometimes, love doesn't stay the way it started. And sometimes, the most loving thing we can do is... let go.

Letting go is not about forgetting.

It's about remembering with peace.

It's not weakness.

It's choosing to heal, grow, and move forward.

"You will know love when it feels like freedom, not a cage."

— Half Me, Half the World

Why Love Hurts Sometimes

- Because we expect it to last forever.

- Because we attach our worth to how others treat us.

- Because we hold on even when it's time to release.

But pain in love doesn't mean the love was fake.

It means it was real—and real things hurt when they change.

Religious Teachings on Love and Detachment

Guru Granth Sahib Ji:

"Jis no premkhelankachao, sir dhar tali gali meriaao."

("If you wish to play the game of love with me, come with your head in your hand.")

— Guru Nanak Dev Ji

True love asks for deep surrender—not possession, but devotion.

Bhagavad Gita:

"Do your duty, but do not cling to its results."

— Chapter 2, Verse 47

This teaches us to love and give without expecting anything in return. That's pure love.

Bible:

"Love is patient, love is kind… it does not envy, it does not boast, it is not proud."

— 1 Corinthians 13:4-5

This kind of love is peaceful, forgiving, and humble—not controlling.

Quran:

"Indeed, those who have believed and done righteous deeds – the Most Merciful will appoint for them affection."

— Surah Maryam 19:96

True love is rooted in kindness, faith, and mercy—not force or control.

From Jordan Peterson (12 Rules for Life):

"Love is the desire to see unnecessary suffering ameliorated."

He reminds us that true love is not just about emotion, but action—wanting the best for someone, even if it's not easy.

The Balloon in the Sky

A young boy held a bright red balloon. He loved it and didn't want to let it go. But the string slipped, and the balloon floated away into the blue sky.

The boy cried.

His grandfather sat beside him and said,

"Sometimes, we must let go of things we love to see how high they can go."

Not everything we love is meant to stay. But everything we love teaches us something.

What Letting Go Looks Like

- Accepting the truth without trying to change it.

- Choosing peace over control.

- Being grateful for the memory, not bitter about the ending.

- Letting go of what was, to make space for what will be.

From The Daily Stoic by Ryan Holiday:

"The obstacle on the path becomes the path. Never forget, within every obstacle is an opportunity to improve our condition."

Letting go is hard. But it becomes the beginning of your healing.

David Goggins on Emotional Pain:

"The most important conversations you'll ever have are the ones you'll have with yourself."

Letting go doesn't just mean moving on from others. Sometimes, it means letting go of the stories we tell ourselves that no longer help us.

A Goodbye Letter

Write a letter to someone or something you need to let go of.

You don't have to send it.

Write what they meant to you.

What you learned.

And say goodbye—not in anger, but with love.

You'll feel lighter after.

Final Words of This Chapter

Love changes us.

Letting go transforms us.

You can love someone and still walk away.

You can forgive and still protect your peace.

You can remember and still move forward.

Half of us is made by love.

The other half is made by the letting go.

And both are beautiful.

Chapter 13: Purpose and the Quiet Voice Inside You

Not Everyone Shouts Their Calling. Some Whisper It.

There's a voice inside you.

It doesn't yell. It doesn't demand attention.

It simply whispers—when you're quiet enough to listen.

This is the voice of purpose—the deep feeling that your life matters, that you're here for a reason beyond just surviving.

Many people spend their whole lives chasing what others tell them to want—money, fame, status. But at night, when the world gets quiet, they feel something's missing.

That missing piece is purpose.

"Your purpose doesn't always shout. Sometimes, it waits for you in silence."

— Half Me, Half the World

What is Purpose, Really?

Purpose isn't a job title.

It's not being famous or rich.

It's the why behind your what.

- A teacher's purpose may not be to finish a syllabus—it's to shape minds.

- A mother's purpose isn't just raising kids—it's building humans with love.

- A writer's purpose isn't selling books—it's connecting souls through words.

Your purpose might be big or quiet. But it is yours, and it gives you meaning.

Religious Teachings on Purpose

Guru Granth Sahib Ji:

"Man tu jot saroop hai, apnamoolpachhaan."

("O my mind, you are the embodiment of the Divine Light – recognize your origin.")

Purpose begins with knowing who you are—divine, powerful, and full of light.

Bhagavad Gita:

"It is better to live your own destiny imperfectly than to live an imitation of somebody else's life with perfection."

— Chapter 3, Verse 35

Your purpose is yours. Don't copy someone else's journey.

Bible:

"For I know the plans I have for you, declares the Lord... plans to prosper you and not to harm you, plans to give you hope and a future."

— Jeremiah 29:11

You are here with intention. Even if you can't see the full path yet.

Quran:

"And I did not create the jinn and mankind except to worship Me."

— SurahAdh-Dhariyat 51:56

Purpose, in Islam, begins with knowing your Creator and serving others with goodness.

From Nietzsche (The Will to Power):

"He who has a why to live can bear almost any how."

A strong sense of purpose helps us endure pain, loss, and confusion. Without purpose, even success feels empty.

A True Story: Helen Keller

Helen Keller was blind and deaf from a young age. The world she lived in was dark and silent. But with the help of her teacher, she learned to speak, read, write, and inspire millions.

Her purpose?

To show the world that no disability can limit a strong spirit.

She once said:

"The only thing worse than being blind is having sight but no vision."

How to Find Your Purpose

1.   Notice what makes you feel alive.

What excites you deeply, even if it's not your job?

2.   Ask yourself: "If I could help the world in one way, what would it be?"

Your gift often lies where your heart breaks.

3.   Don't wait for it to be perfect.

Start small. Purpose grows with action.

4.   Be patient.

Some people find it at 15. Others at 50. What matters is listening.

The Power of Now (EckhartTolle):

"Don't seek your purpose in the future. Your purpose is to be fully present now."

Being present is a purpose in itself—it helps you hear your inner truth.

The "Why" Exercise

Write down:

- What you love doing

- What others come to you for

- What breaks your heart in the world

- What you'd do even if no one paid you

Somewhere in those answers, your purpose is waiting.

Final Words of This Chapter

The world doesn't need you to be like everyone else.

It needs you to be you. Fully. Authentically. Fearlessly.

Purpose is not found in the noise.

It is born in silence, shaped by experience, and lived through courage.

Listen to that quiet voice inside you.

It may be whispering now, but if you follow it—it will lead you somewhere powerful.

Chapter 13: Purpose and the Quiet Voice Inside You

Not Everyone Shouts Their Calling. Some Whisper It.

There's a voice inside you.

It doesn't yell. It doesn't demand attention.

It simply whispers—when you're quiet enough to listen.

This is the voice of purpose—the deep feeling that your life matters, that you're here for a reason beyond just surviving.

Many people spend their whole lives chasing what others tell them to want—money, fame, status. But at night, when the world gets quiet, they feel something's missing.

That missing piece is purpose.

"Your purpose doesn't always shout. Sometimes, it waits for you in silence."

— Half Me, Half the World

What is Purpose, Really?

Purpose isn't a job title.

It's not being famous or rich.

It's the why behind your what.

• A teacher's purpose may not be to finish a syllabus—it's to shape minds.

•	A mother's purpose isn't just raising kids—it's building humans with love.

•	A writer's purpose isn't selling books—it's connecting souls through words.

Your purpose might be big or quiet. But it is yours, and it gives you meaning.

Religious Teachings on Purpose

Guru Granth Sahib Ji:

"Man tu jot saroop hai, apnamoolpachhaan."

("O my mind, you are the embodiment of the Divine Light – recognize your origin.")

Purpose begins with knowing who you are—divine, powerful, and full of light.

Bhagavad Gita:

"It is better to live your own destiny imperfectly than to live an imitation of somebody else's life with perfection."

— Chapter 3, Verse 35

Your purpose is yours. Don't copy someone else's journey.

Bible:

"For I know the plans I have for you, declares the Lord... plans to prosper you and not to harm you, plans to give you hope and a future."

— Jeremiah 29:11

You are here with intention. Even if you can't see the full path yet.

Quran:

"And I did not create the jinn and mankind except to worship Me."

— SurahAdh-Dhariyat 51:56

Purpose, in Islam, begins with knowing your Creator and serving others with goodness.

From Nietzsche (The Will to Power):

"He who has a why to live can bear almost any how."

A strong sense of purpose helps us endure pain, loss, and confusion. Without purpose, even success feels empty.

A True Story: Helen Keller

Helen Keller was blind and deaf from a young age. The world she lived in was dark and silent. But with the help of her teacher, she learned to speak, read, write, and inspire millions.

Her purpose?

To show the world that no disability can limit a strong spirit.

She once said:

"The only thing worse than being blind is having sight but no vision."

How to Find Your Purpose

1.   Notice what makes you feel alive.

What excites you deeply, even if it's not your job?

2.	Ask yourself: "If I could help the world in one way, what would it be?"

Your gift often lies where your heart breaks.

3.	Don't wait for it to be perfect.

Start small. Purpose grows with action.

4.	Be patient.

Some people find it at 15. Others at 50. What matters is listening.

 The Power of Now (EckhartTolle):

"Don't seek your purpose in the future. Your purpose is to be fully present now."

Being present is a purpose in itself—it helps you hear your inner truth.

The "Why" Exercise

Write down:

- What you love doing

- What others come to you for

- What breaks your heart in the world

- What you'd do even if no one paid you

Somewhere in those answers, your purpose is waiting.

Final Words of This Chapter

The world doesn't need you to be like everyone else.

It needs you to be you. Fully. Authentically. Fearlessly.

Purpose is not found in the noise.

It is born in silence, shaped by experience, and lived through courage.

Listen to that quiet voice inside you.

It may be whispering now, but if you follow it—it will lead you somewhere powerful.

Chapter 14: Pain, Struggle, and the Beauty of Endurance

Not All Storms Come to Break You—Some Come to Build You

Pain is something all of us face.

Some face it early. Some later.

Some hide it with a smile. Others let it fall through tears.

But no one escapes it.

This chapter is not about avoiding pain.

It's about understanding it—how struggle can shape us, how wounds can become wisdom, and how suffering, when faced with courage, often gives birth to strength.

"Pain is not just something we go through. Sometimes, it's something we grow through."

— Half Me, Half the World

Why Pain is Part of Life

- Because life is change, and change often hurts.

- Because growth requires discomfort.

- Because deep joy and deep pain often come from the same place—the heart.

We can't remove all pain from life. But we can choose how we face it.

Religious Teachings on Suffering

Guru Granth Sahib Ji:

"Dukhdaru sukh rogbhaia, ja sukh taam na hoi."

(Pain is the medicine, pleasure the disease—where there is pleasure, God is forgotten.)

Suffering can wake us up, guide us, and turn us back to truth.

Bible:

"Not only so, but we also glory in our sufferings, because we know that suffering produces perseverance; perseverance, character; and character, hope."

— Romans 5:3-4

Pain builds patience. Struggle builds character.

Bhagavad Gita:

"Be steadfast in yoga, O Arjuna. Perform your duty and abandon all attachment to success or failure."

— Chapter 2, Verse 48

Even in difficulty, doing your duty with detachment brings peace.

Quran:

"Verily, with hardship comes ease."

— SurahAsh-Sharh 94:6

Hardships are never permanent. Relief always follows.

From Viktor Frankl (Man's Search for Meaning):

"In some way, suffering ceases to be suffering at the moment it finds a meaning."

Frankl survived the Holocaust. He found meaning in unimaginable pain by choosing to help others find purpose, even in the darkest moments.

: Thomas Edison

Edison failed over 1,000 times before inventing the lightbulb.

When asked how it felt to fail so often, he said:

"I have not failed. I've just found 1,000 ways that won't work."

Struggle didn't stop him. It shaped him.

David Goggins on Endurance

"You are in danger of living a life so comfortable and soft, that you will die without ever realizing your true potential."

Goggins turned his pain into power.

He ran when his legs hurt. He trained when his mind resisted.

Pain became his teacher—not his enemy.

: The Pain Journal

- Write about a difficult moment in your life.

- What did it teach you?

- How did you change after that moment?

- Who did you become because of it?

You'll start to see that pain wasn't just a dark chapter. It was a turning point.

From Stoicism (Seneca):

"Difficulties strengthen the mind, as labor does the body."

Pain is the weight you lift to build a stronger soul.

Final Words of This Chapter

You don't have to be fearless to survive pain.

You just have to keep going—one step at a time.

Your scars are not signs of weakness.

They are proof that you stayed when it hurt.

You kept walking when it burned.

And you grew stronger because of it.

The beauty of endurance is not just surviving the storm—

It's learning to dance in the rain.

Chapter 15: The Art of Stillness and the Power of the Present Moment

Sometimes, Doing Nothing is the Most Powerful Thing You Can Do

We live in a world that worships speed.

Always running. Always reaching.

Chasing the next task, the next message, the next goal.

But in all this running... we often miss the moment we're living in.

Stillness is not laziness.

It's a deep strength—a space where clarity begins, where peace grows, and where you finally hear the voice within.

"You're not lost. You're just too busy to hear yourself."

— Half Me, Half the World

Why the Present Moment Matters

- The past is memory.

- The future is imagination.

- Only now is real.

Stillness lets you feel your breath, hear your thoughts, and reconnect with your soul. It's not escape—it's return.

Religious Teachings on Stillness and Presence

Guru Granth Sahib Ji:

"Sahib meraneetnavaa, sadasadadaataar."

(My Lord is forever new, always present and giving.)

God is not in the past or future—He is here, now. When you are present, you are with Him.

Bhagavad Gita:

"When the mind, restrained from wandering, becomes still, one realizes the Self and is content in the Self."

— Chapter 6, Verse 20

True peace is not found outside. It's found in the stillness of your own being.

Bible:

"Be still, and know that I am God."

— Psalm 46:10

Stillness is where divine presence is felt.

Quran:

"Indeed, in the remembrance of Allah do hearts find rest."

— Surah Ar-Ra'd 13:28

Stillness, prayer, and remembrance bring peace to the heart.

EckhartTolle (The Power of Now):

"Realize deeply that the present moment is all you ever have."

Most of our stress comes from either the past we can't change, or the future we can't control. Stillness is the freedom from both.

The Lake and the Mud

A monk asked his students to bring a bowl of water and stir mud into it.

Then he said, "Now, wait."

After a while, the mud settled. The water became clear.

He smiled and said, "This is your mind. When it is still, it sees clearly."

From Stoicism (Marcus Aurelius):

"Nowhere you can go is more peaceful than the place within yourself."

The Stoics believed that no matter how chaotic the world gets, peace is always possible—inside.

A One-Minute Presence Practice

1.	Close your eyes.

2.	Take 3 deep breaths.

3.	Notice the feeling of air entering your nose, and leaving.

4.	Listen to your heartbeat, or the sounds around you.

5.	Do nothing—just be.

Even one minute of presence can calm the storm inside.

Osho (The Book of Man):

"Meditation is not something you do. It is something you fall into when you stop doing."

Osho reminds us: the most powerful moments are often silent. When you stop chasing, life starts flowing.

Final Words of This Chapter

You don't have to fight every battle.

You don't have to rush every step.

Sometimes, the greatest strength is sitting in silence and letting the world slow down.

Stillness is where your soul speaks.

The present moment is where your life actually happens.

Don't just exist—experience.

Don't just chase time—touch it.

Chapter 16: Voices of the World — What We Learn From Others

You Are Not Alone in This Journey

You are half you, but you're also half the world.

The world doesn't just surround you—it shapes you.

Every person you meet, every book you read, every story you hear leaves a mark on your soul.

Some open your heart. Some challenge your thinking.

Some hurt you… and some heal you.

Learning from others isn't weakness. It's wisdom.

"Every face you meet is a mirror. Every voice you hear is a teacher."

— Half Me, Half the World

Why Other People Matter

• They show us who we are. Sometimes we only see ourselves clearly through someone else's eyes.

• They show us who we could be. Role models light the path we never saw.

• They teach us through their mistakes. Every life carries lessons—if we're willing to listen.

Religious Teachings About Learning from Others

Guru Granth Sahib Ji:

"Gurkeshabad mere mitra, dukhsabhbhagae har."

(The Guru's words are my friend; they take away all sorrow.)

The teachings of saints, sages, and seekers become guiding voices in our darkest moments.

Bible:

"As iron sharpens iron, so one person sharpens another."

— Proverbs 27:17

We grow stronger by learning from one another.

Bhagavad Gita:

"Approach a teacher with humility, question them, and serve them. The wise will give you knowledge."

— Chapter 4, Verse 34

Wisdom is passed from soul to soul through respect and curiosity.

Quran:

"And We have certainly created man and We know what his soul whispers to him... and We are closer to him than his jugular vein."

— SurahQaf 50:16

Even through others, Allah's wisdom can reach us. Every voice can carry divine insight.

Lessons from Great Lives

Mahatma Gandhi

He said, "Be the change you wish to see in the world."

He didn't shout. He didn't rule. He simply lived truth and love so loudly that the world followed.

Nelson Mandela

27 years in prison didn't break him.

He forgave his enemies and united a nation.

His story teaches us: Forgiveness is power, not weakness.

Anne Frank

A teenage girl hiding from war wrote:

"In spite of everything, I still believe people are really good at heart."

Even in fear, she found hope.

From the Book Mindset by Carol Dweck:

"People with a growth mindset believe they can learn anything—not because they're already smart, but because they're willing to learn."

Learning from others starts with humility. You don't have to know everything—you just need to stay open.

: The "Wisdom List" Exercise

Write down the names of:

- 3 people who have inspired you

- •   3 people who taught you something through failure

- •   3 strangers (authors, speakers, etc.) who've changed how you think

Ask yourself:

What did they teach me? What part of them lives in me now?

You'll realize—you're not alone. The world has always been teaching you.

: The Two Pots

A water-bearer had two pots. One was cracked and leaked water.

Every day, the pot felt ashamed of losing water on the path.

One day, the bearer smiled and said:

"Look back. See the flowers growing on your side of the path? I planted seeds, and your drops watered them every day."

Lesson: Even our flaws teach someone else something beautiful.

Final Words of This Chapter

Listen. Watch. Ask.

The world is always speaking to you—through people, stories, challenges, and grace.

Your journey is yours, but you are never walking alone.

Every soul you meet... carries a piece of your answer.

Chapter 17: Love, Loss, and the Lessons in Between

Love Isn't Just a Feeling—It's a Teacher

We all seek love.

We give it.

We lose it.

And sometimes, we don't realize how much we've learned from it until much later.

Love is not just something that makes us happy—it changes us.

It shapes the way we see the world, how we treat others, and even how we understand ourselves.

"Love teaches us to give without expecting. Loss teaches us to cherish what remains."

— Half Me, Half the World

The Power of Love

Love is often thought of as something sweet and soft—something that feels good.

But love is also powerful, difficult, and sometimes painful. It can stretch you, change you, and force you to grow.

- Love makes us vulnerable.

When you love deeply, you open yourself up to pain. But you also open yourself to joy.

- Love teaches patience.

It shows you how to wait, how to compromise, and how to put someone else's needs above your own.

- Love connects us to others.

Love teaches us that we are not alone, that we share something deeply human with everyone we meet.

Religious Teachings on Love

Guru Granth Sahib Ji:

"Ik Onkar, Satnam, KartaPurakh, Nirbhau, Nirvair."

(God is One. His Name is Truth. He is the Creator, Fearless, and Without Enmity.)

Love, in Sikhism, is seen as the force that unites us with God and with one another. True love transcends fear and hatred. It is the highest form of devotion.

Bible:

"Love is patient, love is kind. It does not envy, it does not boast, it is not proud."

— 1 Corinthians 13:4

This passage reminds us that love isn't just a feeling—it's an action, a choice we make every day.

Bhagavad Gita:

"The one who loves all beings as his own self, and who is without hatred, is said to have reached the supreme goal."

— Chapter 12, Verse 18

True love goes beyond attachment—it's a selfless act of giving, seeing the Divine in everyone.

Quran:

"And those who believe are stronger in love for Allah."

— SurahAl-Baqarah 2:165

The love for God and His creations is seen as the highest form of love in Islam.

Love and Loss: The Two Sides of the Same Coin

In life, we don't only encounter love—we also face its opposite: loss.

Loss can be devastating, but it is also one of the most profound teachers.

When we lose something we love—whether it's a person, a dream, or a part of ourselves—we learn lessons we never could have learned otherwise.

A Mother's Love

When a mother loses her child, it's often said that the world stops.

Yet, some mothers, even through their tears, find ways to help others.

A mother's love never fades, even in the face of loss. It becomes a source of strength for those who witness it.

Lessons from Love and Loss

The Power of Presence

Loving someone deeply means being there in the hard moments, not just the easy ones. When you are present, you show love even without words.

Sometimes, the greatest gift you can give someone is your attention.

The Gift of Letting Go

Loving isn't always holding on. Sometimes, it's knowing when to let go. Whether it's a friendship, a relationship, or a dream, letting go allows space for new beginnings.

From Man's Search for Meaning by Viktor Frankl:

"Those who have a 'why' to live, can bear with almost any 'how'."

Frankl lost his family in the Holocaust, yet he found a way to move forward. His love for life, and for those he had lost, became his driving force.

The Love and Loss Letter

- Write a letter to someone you love, but can't be with.

- Express all the things you've never said to them.

- Let the love flow, and then the loss.

- Then, write a letter to yourself, about what you've learned from loving them.

The Broken Vase

There once was a beautiful vase. Over time, it cracked and broke. The owner, heartbroken, threw it away.

Years later, he found another vase—this time, an even more beautiful one. But it was the cracks in the old vase that helped him appreciate the new one. The past pain had made room for new joy.

Final Words of This Chapter

Love isn't just a feeling.

It's a teacher, a healer, and sometimes, a guide through pain.

Loss isn't the end—it's a part of the journey. Through it, we understand that nothing is permanent, and everything is precious.

Love deeply. Lose gracefully.

And in the end, we find that love has shaped us more than we ever imagined.

Chapter 18: Courage and Fear — The Dance of Life

Fear is the Shadow; Courage is the Light

We all feel fear.

It's a natural part of life.

Fear is like a shadow—it follows us, whispers doubts, and sometimes paralyzes us.

But courage is the light that cuts through the darkness.

It doesn't erase fear, but it allows us to face it, understand it, and move through it.

"Courage is not the absence of fear, but the strength to act despite it."

— Half Me, Half the World

Why Fear Exists

Fear exists because we're alive.

It's there to protect us.

But sometimes, it overreacts—it makes mountains out of molehills, turning small challenges into overwhelming obstacles.

Fear isn't something to eliminate. It's something to understand.

When we face fear with courage, we turn it into a tool for growth.

The Power of Courage

- Courage means moving forward.

Even when you're scared, courage is taking one more step. It's not about being fearless—it's about not letting fear stop you.

- Courage means acting on your beliefs.

When you have a purpose, courage comes naturally. It's the fuel that lets you stay true to what you believe—even when others doubt you.

- Courage means speaking the truth.

It takes courage to stand up for what's right, especially when it's easier to stay silent. But the world changes when people find the courage to speak.

Religious Teachings on Courage

Guru Granth Sahib Ji:

"Nanak naamchardi kala, terebhanesarbat da bhala."

(Guru Nanak said: With God's name, let the spirit of optimism and courage rise in us.)

Sikhism teaches that courage comes from the Divine. When we trust in God, we gain the strength to face anything.

Bible:

"Be strong and courageous. Do not be afraid; do not be discouraged, for the Lord your God will be with you wherever you go."

— Joshua 1:9

In times of fear, God's presence is the greatest source of courage.

Bhagavad Gita:

"The one who is fearless, who has a strong mind, and who sees everything equally, is the true warrior."

— Chapter 2, Verse 19

Courage is not about defeating others, but conquering the fears within.

Quran:

"And when you are met with a blow, remember that you have the strength to rise again."

— SurahAsh-Sharh 94:5-6

Strength and courage come when we remember our resilience in the face of hardship.

: The Young Warrior

In the days of old, there was a young prince who feared the war his kingdom was going to fight. He prayed for strength, but no answer came. Then, his teacher told him, "Fear isn't your enemy. It's your teacher. Face it and grow stronger."

The prince went to battle, not without fear, but with the courage to fight despite it—and became a hero.

From The Will to Power by Friedrich Nietzsche:

"He who has a why to live can bear almost any how."

When we know what we stand for, the challenges we face become smaller. Courage arises when we find our "why."

: The Fear List

Write down 3 things you fear most.

Then, write down how facing each fear might change your life.

Ask yourself:

What's the worst that could happen? And is it really as bad as I imagine?

A Simple Story: The Fear of the Dark

There was once a child afraid of the dark. Every night, he would cry for his mother.

One day, his mother asked him, "What do you fear about the dark?"

The child said, "It's just... so unknown. I don't know what's there."

The mother smiled and said, "But the dark isn't empty. It's just a space waiting for you to fill it with light."

The child became less afraid the more he embraced the dark. And he discovered that the light inside him could shine brighter in the dark.

From Thinking, Fast and Slow by Daniel Kahneman:

"We're wired to feel fear. But we're also capable of thinking through it."

Our brains often overreact to fear. With practice, we can slow down and think clearly about what's really at stake.

The Courage to Fail

Failure isn't the opposite of courage. It's a part of courage.

The true test of courage is not in avoiding failure, but in getting back up after it.

When we fall, we learn. When we rise, we grow.

Final Words of This Chapter

Fear is real, but it doesn't have to control you.

Courage isn't the absence of fear—it's the willingness to walk through it, to face it head-on, and to grow from it.

Face your fears, embrace the unknown, and let courage be your guide.

Chapter 19 : The Quiet Victories

"The biggest battles are the ones no one sees — fought in silence, won with strength."

1. The Fights No One Talks About

Every day, people around us are fighting battles we know nothing about.

A student smiles in school but goes home to silence.

A mother laughs with her children while hiding her tears at night.

A friend cracks jokes in a group chat but cries alone in their room.

These are quiet victories. There is no applause, no trophy, no spotlight. And yet, they are some of the strongest moments a human can live through.

2. Not All Strength Is Loud

We grow up thinking strength means lifting heavy weights or speaking loudly in a room. But real strength is quiet.

It's choosing not to reply with anger.

It's staying kind when the world is cruel.

It's waking up and trying again when your heart feels broken.

My grandmother, Gurjeet Kaur, once told me, "Being strong doesn't mean showing off your strength. It means surviving without needing to prove it."

Those words never left me.

3. The Story of Aman

Aman was in his final year of college. He looked like a normal guy — laughed with friends, studied hard, even helped others with assignments.

What no one knew was that Aman was working night shifts to support his family. His father had lost his job. His mother was unwell. Every evening after classes, Aman worked as a delivery boy till midnight.

One day, his friend found out and asked, "Why didn't you tell anyone?"

Aman simply said, "Because this is my fight. Not everyone needs to see the war I'm fighting."

That's what quiet victory looks like — doing what's right without needing to be seen.

4. When You Choose to Keep Going

There are days when just waking up is hard.

When your mind is heavy, and your heart is tired.

When everything feels slow, empty, and pointless.

But you still get up. You brush your teeth. You face the world. Even with fear in your chest and sadness in your bones, you keep going.

That — more than anything — is courage.

5. The World May Not Applaud You — But I Will

The world doesn't always clap when you do the right thing.

It doesn't reward you for healing quietly.

But today, I want to say this — if you're still here, still trying, still breathing through your pain — I see you.

I applaud you.

You are not weak. You are powerful beyond words.

6. Healing Happens in Small Steps

You don't have to fix everything in one day.

Healing is in the little moments:

- Making your bed when you don't feel like it.

- Drinking water when your mind is clouded.

- Texting a friend back even when you feel numb.

- Writing in a journal when your heart is heavy.

These are all victories. Small, silent, but powerful.

7. Remember This

Not all victories are loud.

Not all battles are visible.

Not all heroes wear medals.

Some wear tired eyes and quiet smiles.

Some cry in the bathroom and still return to their families with warmth.

Some struggle every morning and still show up for their dreams.

If that's you — I'm proud of you.

8. A Note to the Reader

You don't have to be perfect.

You don't have to have it all figured out.

Take it one moment at a time.

You are doing better than you think.

You are stronger than you believe.

And your quiet victories?

They matter.

"Every step you take, even the small ones, is still movement. And movement is proof — proof that you haven't given up."

Chapter 20: Becoming Your Own Home

"The person you're becoming is worth protecting — even if it means walking alone for a while."

— Jagat Sandhu

1. The Loneliness You Can't Explain

There are days when everything feels heavy — and you don't even know why.

You wake up tired. You scroll through your phone but feel disconnected. You're surrounded by people, yet you feel completely alone.

This is the kind of loneliness that doesn't come from being without others — it comes from feeling disconnected from yourself.

You try to distract yourself — music, movies, talking to friends. But deep inside, there's a space that feels empty.

And the truth is: only you can fill that space.

2. Learning to Sit With Yourself

At first, it's uncomfortable.

Being alone with your thoughts feels strange.

Your mind runs in circles.

Memories come back.

Regrets whisper.

Doubts scream.

But the more you sit with yourself, the more you learn to listen — not to the noise, but to your own heart.

You begin to understand what makes you sad, what brings you peace, what you truly need.

And slowly, your own presence starts to feel like safety — not punishment.

3. You Are Not Incomplete

We've been taught to believe we need someone else to "complete" us — a partner, a friend, a soulmate.

But the truth is: you were never incomplete.

People can add joy, support, and love to your life — but you are whole already.

The more you rely on yourself emotionally, the more powerful you become. Not because you don't need people — but because you don't fear being without them.

4. The Story of Simran

Simran was 24 when she faced the hardest year of her life. Her relationship ended. Her best friend moved away. Her job became stressful.

She cried often. Ate less. Spoke little.

One day, she took a bus to a hill town alone. No plan. No reason. Just her backpack and silence.

She spent a week alone — walking, writing, thinking. She started feeling emotions she had buried for years.

When she returned, she didn't "fix" her life immediately. But she came back stronger — not because someone saved her, but because she saved herself.

5. Becoming Your Own Friend

Start by being kind to yourself.

- Talk to yourself the way you'd talk to a friend.

- Stop calling yourself "stupid," "lazy," or "not enough."

- Celebrate your smallest wins.

- Be gentle with your mistakes.

You've been surviving so much — silently. That deserves kindness, not criticism.

The longest relationship you'll ever have is with yourself. Make it a loving one.

6. Boundaries Are a Form of Self-Love

Loving yourself also means knowing when to say:

- "No, I can't do that today."

- "This is hurting me, and I need space."

- "I deserve better."

Setting boundaries doesn't make you selfish. It makes you safe.

You are not here to constantly please others at the cost of your peace. You are here to live honestly, with love — starting with love for yourself.

7. You're Growing, Even If It Doesn't Show

Growth isn't always loud.

It doesn't always look like new jobs, new goals, or big wins.

Sometimes it looks like:

- Crying and still getting up.

- Choosing peace over proving your point.

- Saying "I need help."

- Not texting that person back.

These are small signs. Quiet signs. But they are proof: you are becoming your own home.

8. Be Proud of How Far You've Come

No one knows the full story of your struggle.

No one sees your silent efforts.

But you do.

You've survived heartbreak.

You've faced fear.

You've healed wounds no one else knew you had.

That is strength. That is something to be proud of.

You don't need anyone else to validate your journey. Just look at the person you've become — softer, wiser, braver.

"One day you'll look back and realize: the love you were searching for... you gave to yourself."

Chapter 21: Finding Peace in a Chaotic World

"Peace isn't a place you reach. It's something you choose — again and again, even when everything around you is loud."

— Jagat Sandhu

1. The Noise We Live In

We live in a world that never stops.

Notifications light up our screens.

News updates shake us.

People's opinions surround us.

Expectations weigh on our shoulders.

It feels like everything demands a response — now, urgently, instantly. We're always doing, replying, explaining, surviving.

But in all this noise, we forget how to just be.

2. The Myth of "When Things Calm Down"

We often tell ourselves:

- "I'll rest when this project ends."
- "I'll find peace after this heartbreak heals."

- "I'll breathe once things settle."

But life rarely gives us a perfect moment. There's always something — deadlines, drama, pain, change.

Peace is not something we wait for.

It's something we learn to create — even in the middle of the storm.

3. A Story From My Grandfather

My grandfather, Nirvail Singh, once told me a story during a power cut. We sat in silence, only the sound of a candle's flame flickering between us.

He said, "When I was young, I wanted life to be quiet so I could think. But as I got older, I learned: the world doesn't get quieter. I had to quiet myself instead."

His words felt like lightning in the dark. Peace wasn't around him — it was inside him.

4. Small Habits That Build Peace

You don't need to escape to the mountains to find peace.

You can begin with simple acts:

- Wake up 10 minutes earlier and sit in silence.

- Turn your phone off during meals.

- Write one line a day about how you feel.

- Breathe deeply before replying in anger.

Peace isn't a big event. It's a small choice — made often, made quietly.

5. Letting Go of What You Can't Control

One of the greatest paths to peace is acceptance.

- You can't control what people say about you.

- You can't change how someone treats you.

- You can't rewrite the past.

But you can choose how much space it takes up in your mind.

Acceptance isn't giving up.

It's letting go of the weight that's not yours to carry anymore.

6. A Letter You'll Never Send

Write a letter you never plan to send.

To the one who hurt you.

To the version of you who made mistakes.

To the memory that still keeps you awake at night.

Say everything. Cry if you must.

Then fold it, and let it go — burn it, tear it, release it.

This is how you reclaim your peace.

Not by changing the past — but by making peace with it.

7. Choosing Stillness

Stillness is not laziness.

Stillness is strength.

In a world that pushes you to be "busy," stillness is rebellion.

When everyone is running, stillness is wisdom.

When your thoughts race, stillness is safety.

Give yourself permission to do nothing sometimes.

To rest. To reflect. To feel.

That's not wasting time — that's healing.

8. You Are Allowed to Protect Your Peace

It's okay to say no.

It's okay to leave that group chat.

It's okay to mute the world and listen to your soul.

You are not a machine.

You are a soul — sensitive, sacred, human.

Your peace is your power. Protect it.

"Even in chaos, you can be calm. Even in noise, you can be quiet. Even in a storm, you can be at peace — not because the world is gentle, but because you've learned how to be."

Chapter 22: Trusting Yourself When No One Else Does

"Sometimes the loudest voice you'll ever need to hear… is your own."

1. When Doubt Comes From Others

They told you your dream was too big.

That your ideas were foolish.

That you weren't strong enough.

Smart enough.

Brave enough.

And maybe, slowly, you started believing them.

But here's the truth: other people don't get to decide your limits. Their doubts don't define your destiny.

2. The Voice That Matters Most

Inside you is a voice — quiet, often ignored, but full of truth.

It's the voice that says:

- "Try again."

- "Keep going."

- "You're not done yet."

When the world is filled with noise, confusion, and criticism, you must turn the volume up on your own inner voice.

The more you listen to yourself, the less you'll need approval from others.

3. The World Needs More People Who Believe in Themselves

Think of the people you admire — writers, athletes, inventors, leaders.

Almost all of them were doubted.

- Walt Disney was fired for "lacking imagination."

- J.K. Rowling was rejected by 12 publishers before Harry Potter got accepted.

- Albert Einstein couldn't speak fluently until he was nine.

If they had believed the world's opinion of them, their light would've gone out early.

Instead, they trusted the spark within — and that spark became a fire.

4. A Story of Fear and Faith

There was a young man who wanted to become a singer. But every time he sang, someone laughed.

He stopped singing for years. Until one day, he was alone on a bus, humming softly to himself. An old woman in the next seat leaned over and said, "You have a gift. Don't hide it."

That stranger reminded him of something he forgot: you don't need everyone to believe in you. Sometimes, just one voice — even your own — is enough.

He started singing again. Years later, he stood on a stage — not because the world gave him permission, but because he gave it to himself.

5. Trust Is Built in Silence

You won't always have cheerleaders.

You won't always have support.

Some dreams will begin in rooms where you sit — completely alone.

But solitude is where self-trust is built.

It's in those quiet moments that you begin to realize:

"I don't need to be loud to be strong."

"I don't need proof to take the first step."

"I can trust my own feet on this path."

6. Mistakes Are Not Evidence Against You

You will mess up.

You will fail.

You will question yourself.

But none of that means you aren't capable.

Every mistake is a stepping stone. Every setback is a message: "This way is not for you. Try another."

Trusting yourself doesn't mean you're always right — it means you're willing to keep learning, growing, and walking forward.

7. The Mirror Test

Look at yourself in the mirror. Not to check your face or your hair — but to ask:

- "Am I proud of how far I've come?"

- "Am I making myself proud?"

- "Do I believe in who I'm becoming?"

If the answer is yes — keep going.

If the answer is no — still keep going. That belief will grow.

The mirror can't lie when your soul is honest.

8. Say This to Yourself Often

- "I know what I'm doing."

- • "I trust myself to figure it out."

- • "Even if I'm scared, I'll try."

- • "I am my own biggest supporter."

Say it. Write it. Repeat it.

You are building the kind of strength that doesn't depend on applause — only on belief.

"Don't wait for the world to clap for you. Clap for yourself. Loudly. Proudly. Often."

Chapter 23: The Power of Second Chances

"You are not your worst day. You are not your biggest mistake. You are every time you chose to begin again."

— Jagat Sandhu

1. Everyone Fails

Failure is not the end — it's proof that you tried.

Everyone fails. Everyone falls. Everyone feels lost.

What separates the defeated from the strong isn't success — it's the willingness to get back up.

Second chances aren't given. Most of the time, you create them.

2. Your Past Is a Chapter, Not a Sentence

We often think:

- "I messed up. That's who I am."

- "I hurt someone. I don't deserve forgiveness."

- "I failed once. I'll never succeed."

But your past is not a prison — it's a classroom. You are allowed to leave it behind after you've learned the lesson.

Your life is not over because of one wrong turn. It just means you need to find a new path.

3. A Letter From the Future You

Imagine this:

The future you — years ahead — writes a letter to you now. It says:

"Thank you for not giving up on me.

Thank you for choosing growth over guilt.

Thank you for trying again, even when you were tired.

Because of you, I became someone I'm proud of."

Let that voice guide you more than the one that says, "You can't come back from this."

4. Forgiving Yourself

We are often kind to others but cruel to ourselves.

We replay old conversations. We punish ourselves for past decisions. We shame ourselves for what we didn't know then.

But you must understand:

- You were doing your best with what you knew.

- You've grown.

- You deserve your own forgiveness.

Forgiveness is how second chances begin.

5. The Story of sahil

Sahil made a decision in anger that changed everything. He lost friends. His family stopped talking to him. For a year, he lived with guilt so heavy it nearly crushed him.

One day, he walked into a community center. He asked if they needed help. He started serving tea. Cleaning floors. Helping children read.

Slowly, he rebuilt his confidence. Slowly, people began to notice the change.

Today, Sahil speaks to young people about his mistakes — not to hide them, but to prove a fall is not the end unless you refuse to rise.

6. You Are Worth Another Try

You don't need anyone's permission to start again.

- You can reapply.

- You can say sorry.

- You can begin your dream again — even at 30, 50, or 70.

There is no shame in trying again. There is only power.

Every sunrise whispers, "Here's another chance."

7. Redefining Success

Success isn't always big. Sometimes, it's:

- Getting out of bed after a hard night.

- Saying sorry and meaning it.

- Trying again even when you're scared.

Don't wait for a perfect moment to give yourself a second chance.

Make today that moment.

Start now — imperfectly, courageously, honestly.

"Fall seven times. Stand up eight. That's how you rewrite your story."

Chapter 24: The People Who Leave and the Lessons They Leave Behind

"Not everyone you lose is a loss. Some people are lessons in human form."

1. When Someone Walks Away

It stings.

The silence after someone leaves can be louder than any goodbye.

You keep checking your phone, expecting a message.

You replay memories and wonder:

"Was it my fault?"

"Did I mean nothing?"

"Why did they leave?"

But the truth is, not everyone is meant to stay.

Some people are only meant to pass through — to show you something, teach you something, and then move on.

2. Not All Departures Are Tragedies

It's easy to mourn the end of a relationship or friendship.

But sometimes, their leaving made space for something better:

- Peace you didn't know you needed.

- Growth you couldn't have done around them.

- Freedom you were too scared to claim.

Not every goodbye is a wound. Some are windows — opening your life to new light.

3. The People Who Were Never Really There

Let's be honest: some people never truly saw you.

They liked the version of you that was useful, funny, helpful — but not the version that was sad, tired, messy, or real.

When you showed your truth, they vanished.

But that's not your loss — that's your revelation.

You don't need people who only love your performance. You need people who love your truth.

4. Holding On Hurts More Than Letting Go

Sometimes we hold on too tightly — not to people, but to memories, "what ifs," and unspoken words.

But holding on keeps you in pain.

Letting go sets you free.

You don't need closure from someone else to heal.

You can give it to yourself:

- "I did my best."

- "I showed up with love."

- "Now, I choose peace."

That is enough.

5. The Story of Leena

Leena was in love for three years. She gave everything — time, trust, tears.

One day, he left without warning.

At first, she broke.

Then, she rebuilt.

She learned to cook again. She went back to school. She made new friends.

Years later, she met him again. He apologized. She smiled — not because she wanted him back, but because she no longer needed him to feel whole.

She had become her own healing.

6. Some People Are Mirrors

They reflect parts of us we didn't know existed.

- A best friend shows you how fun life can be.

- A partner reveals your fears and your love.

- A stranger reminds you of kindness.

Even those who hurt you teach you something:

- What you deserve.

- What you should never tolerate.

- What wounds still need healing.

Let them go with gratitude, not bitterness.

Chapter 25: Us — The Power of Connection

"In the end, it's not about me or you. It's about us — and what we build together."

— Jagat Sandhu

1. The Need to Belong

Every human being carries a quiet ache:

The ache to be seen.

The ache to be understood.

The ache to feel that they matter.

We are not built to survive alone. We are built to connect — to form bonds deeper than words, stronger than silence.

"We're all just walking each other home."

— Ram Dass, Be Here Now

2. Alone Is a Place, Not a Person

There are times when you'll feel isolated — even in a crowd.

Times when no one seems to hear your pain.

Times when the world feels too loud and you feel too invisible.

But that doesn't mean you're broken. It means you're human.

The truth is, there's someone — maybe someone you haven't met yet — who feels the same.

And your voice might be the one that tells them: "Me too. I get it. I'm here."

3. The Bonds That Change Us

Some people come into your life and everything shifts.

They don't fix you.

They don't save you.

But they see you — fully. And in that seeing, you become more of yourself.

That's the magic of "us."

Two people, neither perfect, helping each other grow.

"It's not the person who breaks you that matters. It's the one who makes you feel whole again."

— The Fault in Our Stars by John Green

4. Building 'Us' Takes Effort

Love is not just feelings.

Friendship is not just fun.

Family is not just blood.

Us — real, lasting "us" — is built with:

- Listening when it's hard.

- Showing up, even when you're tired.

- Apologizing first.

- Choosing each other again and again.

It's not always easy. But it's always worth it.

5. When "Us" Breaks

Sometimes, we lose the people we thought we'd never lose.

We try to fix it.

We cry.

We blame ourselves.

We remember the laughter, the comfort, the memories.

But even if it ends, "us" still mattered.

Not all connections are forever — but they are always formative.

You carry a piece of them.

And they carry a piece of you.

6. A Story of Reconnection

Two friends — Aarav and Kabir — were inseparable in childhood. Time and life separated them.

Ten years passed. One message, one reunion, one honest conversation — and the wall between them dissolved.

They realized: real bonds don't disappear. They just wait patiently for your courage.

7. The Strength of Standing Together

When we fight for something bigger than ourselves — equality, justice, love — us becomes a force.

It's not about one voice yelling.

It's about many voices harmonizing.

"We may have all come on different ships, but we're in the same boat now."

— Martin Luther King Jr.

Together, we are louder. Braver. Kinder.

"You don't need a thousand people. You just need a few who truly get you."

Chapter 26: The Mountain Is You

"You are not facing the mountain. You are the mountain — your own greatest obstacle, and your greatest strength."

1. The Inner Fight

Most of the battles we fight are not with the world — but with ourselves.

- The voice that says "You're not good enough."

- The doubt that whispers "You'll fail again."

- The fear that convinces you to quit before starting.

We wait for someone to rescue us. But the truth is: we must rescue ourselves.

"The only thing standing between you and your goal is the story you keep telling yourself."

— The Mountain Is You by Brianna Wiest

2. Becoming Your Own Enemy

We sabotage ourselves more than anyone else ever could.

- We delay dreams out of fear.

- We shrink our light so others feel comfortable.

- We replay mistakes until they become our identity.

But self-sabotage isn't weakness — it's usually unhealed fear.

And healing starts by recognizing:

You can't defeat what you're still protecting.

3. What Are You Afraid Of?

The fear of failure.

The fear of judgment.

The fear of not being enough.

These are the invisible chains we carry — and they make us tired, small, stuck.

To break them, we must ask hard questions:

- What am I avoiding?

- Who told me I wasn't enough?

- What would I do if I wasn't afraid?

"I am not afraid of storms, for I am learning how to sail my ship."

— Little Women by Louisa May Alcott

4. The Choice to Rise

Every day, you have two choices:

- Stay in the pain of the past.

- Or rise into the power of your potential.

Climbing your mountain won't be easy — but it will be worth it.

Each small step matters. Each choice to try again is sacred.

And every scar you carry is not shame — it's proof of your courage.

5. The Story of Riya

Riya was her own harshest critic. No one judged her more than she judged herself.

She kept telling herself:

- "I'll never be enough."

- "People like me don't succeed."

- "What if I fail again?"

Until one day, exhausted and fed up, she asked herself:

"What if I'm wrong?"

She started applying for jobs. Speaking her mind. Creating art again.

And the world responded — not because she was perfect, but because she finally believed in her right to try.

6. You Are the Mountain. And the Climber.

It sounds strange, but it's true:

You are both the wall you hit and the person strong enough to climb it.

You are not too late. You are not too damaged. You are not behind.

The mountain isn't there to stop you.

It's there to teach you how to rise.

"It's your road, and yours alone. Others may walk it with you, but no one can walk it for you."

— Rumi

"Stop waiting for the world to clear the path. Start becoming the person who walks through fire."

Chapter 27: When It Hurts, Write

"Some wounds don't bleed. They write themselves out through your hands."

— Jagat Sandhu

1. Pain Has a Language

There are times when words fail.

You feel a lump in your throat. A storm in your chest.

And you don't know how to explain it.

That's when writing saves you.

When you put pain into words, it loses power. It becomes shapeable, understandable.

Writing is not just expression — it is extraction. You pull the poison out of your mind and bleed it onto the page.

"You must stay drunk on writing so reality cannot destroy you."

— Fahrenheit 451 by Ray Bradbury

2. Your Journal Is Your Mirror

When no one understands you, your journal does.

It listens without judgment.

It accepts every contradiction inside you.

It becomes the safest place to fall apart.

And slowly, through the mess of thoughts and tears and truths —

you begin to see yourself clearly.

Not the broken version. The real one. The evolving one.

3. Writing Doesn't Have to Be Beautiful

You don't need fancy words. You don't need perfect grammar.

You just need honesty.

Let it be messy. Let it ramble. Let it scream.

The purpose isn't perfection — it's release.

Write like:

- No one will ever read it.

- Your life depends on it.

- You are speaking to the version of you that needed saving five years ago.

"Write hard and clear about what hurts."

— Ernest Hemingway

4. The Words That Stayed

Some of the world's greatest books were born from pain:

- "The Bell Jar" by Sylvia Plath

- "Man's Search for Meaning" by Viktor Frankl

- "Night" by Elie Wiesel

These weren't just books. They were battles.

Proof that words can carry suffering — and transform it.

If they could do it, so can you.

5. Healing Is a Sentence at a Time

Every time you write, you give yourself space to breathe.

One line becomes a truth.

One truth becomes a breakthrough.

One breakthrough becomes freedom.

You might not notice the change immediately. But over time, the pages become lighter.

Because you are becoming lighter too.

6. A Story of Healing Through Writing

Karan was never good at talking. He bottled everything. The pressure made him numb.

One day, in the middle of a breakdown, he opened a notebook and wrote:

"I don't want to feel like this anymore."

That one line led to twenty pages. And those twenty pages became a habit.

Years later, he wasn't just surviving — he was publishing his first poetry collection.

He didn't just write words. He wrote himself back together.

7. Make It a Ritual

Write every day — even if it's one line.

Make it a place you return to when:

- You're confused.

- You're angry.

- You're joyful.

- You feel nothing.

Make writing your way of knowing yourself.

"Words can be like X-rays if you use them properly — they'll go through anything."

— Aldous Huxley, Brave New World

"Writing is the way I try to make sense of the world and myself."

-Jagat sandhu

Chapter 28: Those Who Stayed

"The ones who stayed — through your silence, through your mess, through your storms — are your home."

— Jagat Sandhu

1. Not Everyone Leaves

In a world where so many walk away,

there are a few who don't.

- They stay when you're quiet.

- They stay when you're breaking.

- They stay when you're not easy to love.

They don't ask for a better version of you.

They choose you as you are — not as you pretend to be.

"Some people arrive and make such a beautiful impact on your life, you can barely remember what life was like without them."

— Anna Taylor

2. Loyalty Is a Quiet Thing

It doesn't scream. It doesn't post stories. It doesn't need applause.

It shows up in the smallest, softest ways:

- A message when you're distant.

- A meal when you're too tired to cook.

- A hug that says "You don't have to explain. I understand."

Real loyalty isn't loud. It's consistent.

3. You Don't Need Many — Just a Few

The world will try to convince you that popularity equals worth.

But ten fake friends can't compare to one real one.

One person who gets you — truly gets you — is worth more than a thousand who don't.

Let go of the need to be liked by everyone.

Instead, protect the rare ones who stay.

"If you have one true friend, you have more than your share."

— Thomas Fuller

4. The People Who Saw You at Your Worst

We all have a moment — a low we don't talk about.

The night we cried until we fell asleep.

The month we felt like giving up.

The year everything fell apart.

If someone stayed through that — they're not just a friend.

They're family by soul.

Keep them close. Thank them often. Don't take them for granted.

5. A Story of Staying

When Simran lost her job, she also lost herself.

She pushed people away. She didn't return calls. She stopped smiling.

But her friend Meher came every week anyway — with food, with kindness, with no expectations.

One day, Simran finally cried in her arms and said,

"Why didn't you give up on me?"

Meher smiled, "Because you would have stayed for me too."

That's what real ones do.

6. Stay for Others Too

Just as others stayed for you — stay for someone else.

- Be the person who answers at 2 a.m.

- Be the friend who notices quiet pain.

- Be the one who stays, even when they push you away.

Not everyone knows how to ask for help.

Sometimes, love is shown by not leaving.

7. The Gift of Being Chosen Again and Again

Real love is not a one-time promise. It's a daily choice.

- "I still believe in you."

- "I still want to walk with you."

- "I still choose you — flaws and all."

And when someone does that for you, remember:

That's the kind of love you always deserved.

"Sometimes we just need someone to simply be there, not to fix anything, but to let us feel we're supported and loved."

"The ones who stay when it's hard are the ones who matter when it's easy."

Chapter 29: The Weight of Expectations

"The expectations we carry are often heavier than the reality we live. Let go, and you'll find freedom."

1. The Invisible Load We Carry

Expectations are like invisible weights we carry on our shoulders every day. From the moment we're born, we're handed a set of expectations—some from our parents, some from society, and some we place on ourselves. You're expected to get good grades, land a prestigious job, marry the "right" person, and live a life that looks successful to others. But what happens when these expectations don't align with who you truly are? What happens when the weight becomes too much to bear?

I remember my own struggle with expectations when I was in high school. My parents wanted me to become an engineer—a stable, respected career. But my heart was drawn to writing. I loved crafting stories, pouring my emotions onto the page, and imagining worlds beyond my own. Every time I mentioned my dream, I'd see the disappointment in my parents' eyes. "Writing won't pay the bills," they'd say. "You need a real job." Their words felt like bricks piling onto my chest. I wanted to make them proud, but I also wanted to be true to myself. The conflict tore me apart for years.

Expectations aren't always external, though. Sometimes, the heaviest ones come from within. We tell ourselves we need to be perfect—perfect students, perfect parents, perfect partners. We scroll through social media, comparing our messy lives to the curated perfection of others, and we feel like we're failing. But here's the truth: expectations are often illusions. They're based on someone else's idea of success, not yours.

2. A Story of Breaking Free

Let me tell you about Priya, a young woman I met during a writing workshop. Priya was the eldest daughter in a traditional family, and from the time she was a child, her parents had one dream for her: to become a doctor. They saw it as the ultimate achievement—a way to secure her future and bring honor to the family. Priya studied hard, aced her exams, and got into medical school. But deep down, she felt empty. Her true passion was painting. She'd spend hours in her room, creating vibrant canvases filled with colors that expressed emotions she couldn't put into words.

One day, Priya's mother found her sketchbook and confronted her. "Why are you wasting time on this?" she asked. "You need to focus on your studies." Priya felt her heart break. She wanted to please her parents, but she also knew she couldn't live a lie. After months of inner turmoil, Priya made a decision. She sat her parents down and said, "I can't be what you want. I need to be what I am." There were tears, arguments, and weeks of silence. But Priya stood her ground. She left medical school and enrolled in an art program.

At first, her parents were devastated. They worried about her future, about what people would say. But over time, they saw how Priya's face lit up when she talked about her art. They saw her talent, her dedication, and eventually, her success. Today, Priya is a renowned artist, not because she met her parents' expectations, but because she broke free from them. Her story taught me that sometimes, the bravest thing you can do is to disappoint others if it means staying true to yourself.

3. Why Expectations Feel So Heavy

Expectations feel heavy because they're often tied to fear—fear of failure, fear of judgment, fear of letting others down. When we live under the weight of expectations, we're not living for ourselves; we're living for someone else's approval. It's exhausting. It's like trying to run a race while carrying a backpack full of rocks. You might keep going for a while, but eventually, you'll collapse.

I've seen this in my own life and in the lives of others. A friend of mine, Rohan, was expected to take over his family's business. He didn't want to—he dreamed of becoming a chef. But the pressure from his family was immense. "You're the only son," they'd say. "This is your responsibility." Rohan tried to follow their path, but he was miserable. He'd come home from the office, cook elaborate meals, and dream of opening his own restaurant. One day, he had a breakdown. He told me, "I feel like I'm living someone else's life." That was the moment he decided to let go of the expectations and pursue his passion. It wasn't easy—he faced criticism and doubt—but today, he runs a successful restaurant, and his family has come to respect his choice.

Expectations can also be self-imposed. We set impossibly high standards for ourselves, thinking that's the only way to be worthy. But perfection is a myth. It's a moving target you'll never hit. The more you chase it, the more you lose sight of what really matters: your own happiness.

4. Religious Teachings on Letting Go

Expectations often come with attachment—attachment to outcomes, to approval, to a certain image of success. Many spiritual traditions teach us to let go of this attachment to find true peace.

Bhagavad Gita:

"Perform your duties without attachment to the results, for attachment causes fear and sorrow."

— Chapter 2, Verse 47

This verse from the Bhagavad Gita reminds us that our job is to act with sincerity, not to cling to what others expect of us. When we let go of attachment to outcomes, we free ourselves from the fear of failure and the burden of expectations.

Guru Granth Sahib Ji:

"Jo kichhkarnaa so karrahe, horkarai na koi."

(Whatever God does, that happens; no one else can do anything.)

This teaching encourages surrender—not in a passive way, but in a way that trusts the universe's plan over society's expectations. When we align with our true purpose, we find peace, even if it means going against the grain.

5. The Cost of Living for Others

Living under the weight of expectations comes at a cost. It costs you your authenticity. It costs you your joy. It costs you the chance to live a life that's truly yours. I've seen people burn out, lose themselves, and wake up one day wondering, "Who am I?" because they spent so long trying to be what others wanted.

I once met a woman named Aisha at a community event. She was a lawyer, successful by all external measures. But she confided in me that she hated her job. "I became a lawyer because my parents wanted me to," she said. "But I always wanted to be a teacher." Aisha spent years living a life that wasn't hers, and it left her feeling empty. Eventually, she made the leap—she quit her job, went back to school, and became a teacher. She told me, "I've never felt more alive." Aisha's story is a reminder that the cost of meeting expectations can be far greater than the cost of breaking them.

6. A Practice to Release Expectations

Here's a simple exercise to help you let go of the expectations weighing you down:

• Step 1: Take a piece of paper and write down three expectations you're carrying that feel heavy. They could be from your family, your culture, or yourself.

• Step 2: For each expectation, ask yourself:

• Is this truly mine, or does it belong to someone else?

• Does this align with who I want to be, or who I think I should be?

• What would happen if I let this go?

• Step 3: If an expectation doesn't serve your true self, cross it out. Then write a new intention that aligns with your heart. For example, if the expectation is "I need to be a doctor to make my parents proud," your new intention might be, "I will pursue a career that brings me joy and allows me to serve others in my own way."

• Step 4: Take a deep breath and visualize yourself releasing the weight of those expectations. Feel your shoulders lighten, your heart open.

7. The Freedom on the Other Side

When you let go of expectations, you step into freedom. You give yourself permission to be who you are, not who you're supposed to be. This doesn't mean you stop caring about others or striving for excellence—it means you redefine success on your own terms.

I think back to my own journey with writing. After years of struggling with my parents' expectations, I finally chose my path. I started writing this book, pouring my heart into every chapter. My parents didn't understand at first, but over time, they saw how much it meant to me. They saw my passion, my purpose. And slowly, they began to support me. Letting go of their expectations didn't mean I lost their love—it meant I gained my own.

Final Words of This Chapter

Expectations can guide us, but they can also trap us. The moment you choose your own path over someone else's vision for you, you step into freedom. Be brave enough to disappoint others if it means being true to yourself. The life you're meant to live is waiting on the other side of those expectations—don't let them hold you back.

Chapter 30: The Power of Gratitude

"Gratitude doesn't change the world around you—it changes the world within you."

1. Finding Light in the Darkest Moments

Gratitude is often misunderstood. We think it's about being thankful when life is good—when you get a promotion, when your family is healthy, when everything is going your way. But true gratitude is a practice for the hard times. It's about finding light in the darkest moments, about seeing the small sparks of goodness even when everything feels heavy.

I learned this lesson during one of the toughest years of my life. I had just lost a close friend to illness, and my own career was crumbling. I felt like the ground beneath me had disappeared. Every day was a struggle to get out of bed. I'd lie there, replaying my grief, wondering how I'd ever feel whole again. One morning, I forced myself to go for a walk. As I sat on a park bench, I noticed a small bird pecking at the ground. Its tiny movements, so full of life, caught my attention. For the first time in weeks, I felt a flicker of peace. I was grateful for that bird, for that moment of stillness. It didn't erase my pain, but it gave me a reason to keep going.

Gratitude in tough times isn't about ignoring your struggles. It's about shifting your focus, even for a moment, to what still exists— small joys, quiet blessings, the simple fact that you're still here, breathing.

2. A Story of Small Joys

Let me tell you about Harjit, an elderly man I met at that same park. Harjit came every morning to feed the birds. He'd sit on a bench, tossing crumbs, a gentle smile on his face. One day, I struck up a conversation with him. He told me he had lost his wife a year ago and was battling loneliness. His children lived far away, and his days felt empty. Yet, he smiled every day. When I asked how he stayed so positive, he said, "I'm grateful for the birds. They remind me I'm still here, still needed. They give me a reason to get up."

Harjit's words stayed with me. His life wasn't easy—he was grieving, isolated, and facing the challenges of old age. But he found joy in the smallest things: the chirping of birds, the warmth of the sun, the feeling of grass under his feet. He didn't need big reasons to be grateful; he found beauty in the ordinary. Harjit taught me that gratitude is a choice—a choice to see what's still good, even when so much feels wrong.

3. Why Gratitude Matters

Gratitude changes the way you see the world. It doesn't erase your problems, but it softens their edges. When you practice gratitude, you train your mind to look for the good, even in the midst of pain. It's like putting on a pair of glasses that highlight the beauty you might otherwise miss.

Science backs this up. Studies have shown that practicing gratitude can reduce stress, improve sleep, and even boost your immune system. But more than that, gratitude heals your heart. It reminds you that you're not alone, that there's still goodness in the world, that you have reasons to keep going. I've seen this in my own life. On days when I feel overwhelmed, I pause and think of three things I'm grateful for. It might be the smell of rain, a kind word from a friend, or the fact that I have a warm bed to sleep in. Those small things ground me—they remind me that life, even with its hardships, is still worth living.

4. Religious Teachings on Gratitude

Gratitude is a cornerstone of many spiritual traditions. It's seen as a way to connect with the divine, to acknowledge the blessings we've been given, and to cultivate peace within ourselves.

Quran:

"If you are grateful, I will surely increase you [in favor]."

— Surah Ibrahim 14:7

This verse teaches that gratitude opens the door to abundance. When we appreciate what we have, we create space for more blessings to flow into our lives—not because we get more things, but because we see more clearly.

Guru Granth Sahib Ji:

"Nanak, naamjapo, simran karo, sukh paavo."

(Nanak says: Chant the Name, remember God, and find peace.)

Gratitude in Sikhism is often expressed through remembrance of God's gifts. When we take a moment to thank the Creator for our breath, our loved ones, our very existence, we find a deep sense of peace.

5. The Ripple Effect of Gratitude

Gratitude doesn't just change you—it changes the people around you. When you express gratitude, you create a ripple effect of positivity. I've seen this in small, everyday moments. Once, I thanked a barista at a coffee shop for her cheerful service. Her face lit up, and she said, "You made my day." That simple act of gratitude lifted her spirits, and I'm sure she passed that positivity on to others.

Gratitude also deepens your relationships. When you tell someone you appreciate them, you strengthen your bond. I make it a habit to thank my friends and family regularly—not just for big things, but for the little ways they show up. I'll text a friend, "Thank you for always listening when I need to vent," or tell my sister, "I'm grateful for how you make me laugh." These small acts of gratitude make them feel seen, and they make me feel more connected.

6. A Gratitude Practice for Hard Days

Here's a simple gratitude practice you can do, especially on days when life feels heavy:

• Step 1: Find a quiet space and take a few deep breaths.

• Step 2: Write down three things you're grateful for. They don't have to be big—maybe the warmth of your coffee, the sound of your child's laughter, or the fact that you made it through the day.

• Step 3: Reflect on why these things matter. For example, "I'm grateful for this coffee because it gives me a moment of calm in a busy morning."

• Step 4: Say a quiet thank you—to the universe, to God, to yourself. Feel the gratitude in your heart.

I've done this practice on some of my darkest days, and it always helps. It doesn't fix everything, but it shifts my perspective. It reminds me that even in the storm, there are still rays of light.

7. Gratitude as a Lifelong Journey

Gratitude isn't a one-time act—it's a lifelong journey. The more you practice it, the more natural it becomes. Over time, you'll find yourself noticing the good in every situation, even the painful ones. You'll start to see your struggles as teachers, your losses as lessons, your pain as a path to growth.

I think back to that tough year when I lost my friend. In the midst of my grief, gratitude became my lifeline. I was grateful for the memories we shared, for the laughter, for the lessons he taught me. I was grateful for the support of my family, for the strangers who showed me kindness, for the small moments of joy that reminded me life goes on. Gratitude didn't take away my pain, but it helped me carry it. It helped me see that even in loss, there is love.

Final Words of This Chapter

Gratitude is a quiet revolution. It doesn't erase pain, but it helps you carry it with grace. It doesn't change the world around you, but it changes the world within you. Look for the small joys— they're the threads that weave a stronger, softer, more hopeful you. Start today, right now. What are you grateful for?

Chapter 31: The Art of Saying No

"Saying no to what doesn't serve you is saying yes to what does."

— Jagat Sandhu

1. The Fear of Disappointing Others

Saying no is one of the hardest things to do. We're wired to please, to fit in, to be liked. We don't want to seem selfish or unkind, so we say yes even when we don't want to. We say yes to extra work, to social events we're too tired for, to favors we don't have the energy to give. But every yes you give to something that drains you is a no to something that could fill you up—your peace, your passions, your true self.

I've struggled with this my whole life. Growing up, I was the "good kid" who always said yes. If a friend needed help, I was there. If a teacher asked for a volunteer, I raised my hand. If my family needed support, I dropped everything. I thought saying yes made me a good person, but over time, I realized it was making me miserable. I was so busy meeting everyone else's needs that I forgot my own. I'd end up exhausted, resentful, and disconnected from myself.

The fear of disappointing others is real. We worry that saying no will make people think less of us, that they'll stop loving us, that we'll be seen as selfish. But here's the truth: saying no isn't about rejecting others—it's about honoring yourself. It's about setting boundaries that protect your well-being, so you can show up as your best self for the people and things that truly matter.

2. A Story of Boundaries

My friend Neha used to be just like me—a chronic people-pleaser. She said yes to everything: extra projects at work, social events she didn't want to attend, favors for friends and family. She thought it made her a good person, but deep down, she was exhausted. She'd come home at the end of the day with nothing left to give—not to herself, not to her dreams. She felt like she was living on autopilot, always doing for others, never for herself.

One day, Neha's boss asked her to take on another project—a massive one that would require late nights and weekends. Neha was already stretched thin, but she felt the familiar pressure to say yes. She didn't want to seem lazy or uncommitted. But as she sat at her desk, overwhelmed and on the verge of tears, something shifted. She realized that if she said yes to this, she'd be saying no to her own mental health, her hobbies, her time with loved ones. For the first time, she said, "I'd love to help, but I can't take this on right now." Her boss was surprised but respected her decision.

At first, Neha felt guilty. She worried she'd let her team down, that they'd think less of her. But over the next few weeks, she noticed something incredible. She had more energy. She started painting again—a hobby she'd abandoned years ago. She spent quality time with her family, laughing and making memories. Saying no to that project gave her the space to say yes to what truly mattered. Neha's story taught me that boundaries aren't selfish—they're sacred.

3. Why Saying No Feels So Hard

Saying no feels hard because we've been conditioned to equate it with failure. From a young age, we're taught to be agreeable, to go along with what others want, to avoid conflict. We're taught that saying yes makes us good, while saying no makes us difficult. But this mindset comes at a cost. When we say yes to everything, we spread ourselves too thin. We lose sight of our own needs, our own dreams. We become a shell of who we're meant to be.

I've seen this in countless people. A colleague of mine, Sameer, used to say yes to every social invitation, even when he was exhausted. He didn't want to miss out, didn't want to seem rude. But he'd come to work drained, unable to focus, snapping at coworkers because he was so overstretched. One day, I asked him, "Why do you keep saying yes when you're so tired?" He paused and said, "I don't know. I guess I'm scared people will stop inviting me if I say no." Sameer's fear was valid, but it was also unfounded. When he started saying no to events that didn't light him up, he found that his true friends respected his boundaries—and he had more energy for the things he actually enjoyed.

Saying no also feels hard because it requires us to confront our own worth. When we say no, we're saying, "My time matters. My energy matters. I matter." And for many of us, that's a radical act. We're so used to putting others first that prioritizing ourselves feels foreign, even wrong. But it's not wrong—it's necessary.

4. Religious Teachings on Balance and Integrity

Many spiritual traditions emphasize the importance of balance and integrity in our commitments. Saying no isn't about being unkind; it's about being honest—honest with yourself and with others.

Bible:

"Let your yes be yes, and your no be no."

— Matthew 5:37

This verse reminds us to be truthful in our words. A yes given out of obligation isn't honest, and it doesn't serve anyone. A no said with integrity is a loving act—it honors your truth and respects the other person's ability to handle it.

Bhagavad Gita:

"Yoga is skill in action."

— Chapter 2, Verse 50

The Gita teaches that true skill lies in acting with balance, not overextending ourselves to the point of breaking. Saying no is a skillful act—it allows us to show up fully for the things we say yes to.

5. The Power of a Well-Placed No

Saying no is powerful. It's a declaration of self-worth, a boundary that protects your peace, a step toward living authentically. When you say no to what doesn't serve you, you create space for what does. You create space for rest, for joy, for the pursuits that light you up. You create space to be the best version of yourself.

I've experienced this in my own life. A few years ago, I was asked to join a committee that I wasn't passionate about. It was a prestigious role, and I knew it would look good on my resume. But I also knew it would take time away from my writing, which was my true calling. I wrestled with the decision for days, worried about missing out, worried about what people would think. But finally, I said no. And you know what? The world didn't end. The committee found someone else, and I had more time to work on this book. That no was a yes to my dreams, and I've never regretted it.

Saying no also sets an example for others. When you model healthy boundaries, you give the people around you permission to do the same. I've seen this with my sister, who used to overcommit to family events. She'd say yes to hosting every gathering, even when she was exhausted. One day, she saw me decline an invitation because I needed rest. Inspired, she started doing the same. She told me, "I never realized I could say no without feeling guilty. Thank you for showing me that." My no didn't just help me—it helped her too.

6. A Practice to Build Your No Muscle

Saying no takes practice, especially if you're not used to it. Here's a step-by-step guide to help you build your "no muscle":

• Step 1: Pause before answering. When someone asks you to do something, don't respond immediately. Say, "Let me think about it and get back to you." This gives you time to check in with yourself.

• Step 2: Ask yourself: Does this align with my values, my goals, my energy right now? If the answer is no, you have your answer.

• Step 3: Practice a simple, kind response. Try, "Thank you for asking, but I can't right now," or "I'd love to help, but I'm stretched too thin." You don't need to overexplain—your no is enough.

• Step 4: Notice how it feels. At first, you might feel guilty or anxious. That's normal. But over time, you'll feel lighter, more empowered, more in control of your life.

Start small. Say no to something low-stakes, like a casual invitation or a minor request. As you get more comfortable, you'll find it easier to say no to bigger things. Your no is a muscle—the more you use it, the stronger it gets.

7. The Freedom of Boundaries

When you master the art of saying no, you step into a new kind of freedom. You free yourself from the pressure to be everything to everyone. You free yourself to focus on what truly matters—your health, your passions, your relationships with the people who lift you up. You free yourself to live a life that's yours, not someone else's.

I think back to Neha's story. After she started saying no, her life transformed. She had time to pursue her love of painting, to rest when she needed to, to be fully present with her family. She told me, "I used to think saying yes made me a good person. But saying no made me a happier one." Her words remind us that boundaries aren't about shutting people out—they're about letting the right things in.

Final Words of This Chapter

Saying no is not rejection—it's protection. It's a way to honor your time, your energy, your truth. The right people will respect your boundaries, and you'll respect yourself more too. Don't be afraid to say no to what doesn't serve you—it's the only way to say yes to what does. Start today. What's one thing you need to say no to?

Chapter 32: The Courage to Be Vulnerable

"Vulnerability is not weakness—it's the birthplace of connection."

— Jagat Sandhu

1. The Walls We Build

We live in a world that praises strength and hides pain. From a young age, we're taught to be tough, to keep our emotions in check, to never let others see us struggle. We build walls around our hearts, thinking they'll protect us. But those walls don't just keep pain out—they keep love out too. Vulnerability—showing your true self, flaws and all—is the key to breaking down those walls. It's scary, yes, but it's also the birthplace of connection, growth, and authenticity.

I used to be terrified of vulnerability. I thought showing my struggles made me weak, that people would judge me or think less of me. So I kept everything inside. If I was hurting, I'd smile through it. If I was scared, I'd pretend I had it all together. But inside, I felt so alone. My walls kept me safe, but they also kept me isolated. It wasn't until I started opening up that I realized vulnerability isn't weakness—it's courage.

2. A Story of Opening Up

I'll never forget the day I met Vikram at a personal development workshop. Vikram was the kind of person who seemed to have it all together—confident, articulate, always smiling. During a group sharing session, we were asked to talk about a challenge we were facing. I expected Vikram to share something light, but instead, he opened up about a struggle that left us all stunned. He admitted that he felt like a failure after losing his business during the pandemic. His voice shook as he spoke, and I could see the fear in his eyes—fear of being judged, fear of being seen as less than.

But something beautiful happened. The room didn't judge him—they embraced him. People thanked him for his honesty, shared their own struggles, and offered support. By the end of the workshop, Vikram had made friends who became his support system. He told me later, "I was so scared to share that part of me, but it was the best thing I ever did. I don't feel alone anymore." Vikram's story showed me the power of vulnerability—it doesn't push people away; it brings them closer.

3. Why Vulnerability Feels So Scary

Vulnerability feels scary because it requires us to let go of control. When we're vulnerable, we're exposing our true selves—our fears, our insecurities, our imperfections. We're saying, "Here I am, as I am," and trusting that we'll be accepted. That's a risk. What if people reject us? What if they use our vulnerability against us? What if they see us as weak? These fears are valid—they come from a primal need to protect ourselves. But they also keep us from the deep connections we crave.

I've seen this fear in action. A friend of mine, Kavita, went through a divorce a few years ago. She was devastated, but she didn't tell anyone—not even her closest friends. She'd show up to gatherings with a smile, pretending everything was fine. But inside, she was crumbling. When I finally asked her how she was doing, she broke down and told me everything. "I didn't want anyone to see me as broken," she said. But when she shared her pain, her friends rallied around her. They didn't see her as broken—they saw her as human. Kavita learned that vulnerability doesn't make you weak—it makes you relatable.

4. The Science and Wisdom of Vulnerability

Brené Brown, a researcher and author, has spent years studying vulnerability. In her book Daring Greatly, she writes:

"Vulnerability is the core of all emotions and feelings. To feel is to be vulnerable."

Brown's research shows that vulnerability is the foundation of courage, creativity, and connection. When we hide our true selves, we also hide our ability to connect deeply with others. But when we're vulnerable, we create space for authenticity, empathy, and love.

I've experienced this firsthand. A few years ago, I was struggling with self-doubt as I wrote this book. I felt like a fraud—who was I to write about life lessons when my own life was so messy? I kept these feelings to myself, but they ate away at me. Finally, I shared them with a close friend. I said, "I'm terrified I'm not good enough to do this." Instead of judging me, my friend hugged me and said, "I feel that way all the time. You're not alone." Her words lifted a weight off my shoulders. My vulnerability didn't make me weaker—it made me stronger, because it connected me to someone who understood.

5. Religious Teachings on Vulnerability

Many spiritual traditions encourage vulnerability as a path to growth and connection. They remind us that we don't have to be perfect—we just have to be real.

Guru Granth Sahib Ji:

"Nanak, dukhvich sukh da mool hai."

(Nanak says: In pain lies the root of peace.)

This teaching reminds us that embracing our struggles—being vulnerable about our pain—leads to true peace. When we stop hiding, we allow healing to begin.

Bible:

"My grace is sufficient for you, for my power is made perfect in weakness."

— 2 Corinthians 12:9

This verse encourages us to embrace our imperfections. When we're vulnerable, we make space for divine grace to work through us.

6. The Rewards of Vulnerability

Vulnerability is a risk, but it comes with incredible rewards. When you're vulnerable, you invite others to be vulnerable too. You create a space where people can show up as their true selves, not as the polished versions they think they need to be. This leads to deeper, more meaningful relationships—relationships built on trust, empathy, and understanding.

I've seen this in my own life. After I started opening up about my struggles, my relationships changed. My friends and family began sharing their own challenges with me. We had honest conversations—about fear, about failure, about dreams—and those conversations brought us closer. Vulnerability didn't make me weaker; it made my connections stronger.

Vulnerability also helps you grow. When you're honest about your struggles, you can face them head-on. You can ask for help, seek solutions, and learn from your experiences. I think back to Vikram's story. By sharing his failure, he not only found support—

he found clarity. He started rebuilding his life, not because he hid his pain, but because he owned it.

7. A Vulnerability Challenge

Here's a challenge to help you practice vulnerability:

• Step 1: Think of someone you trust—a friend, a family member, a partner.

• Step 2: Share something real with them. It could be a fear ("I'm scared I'll never achieve my dreams"), a struggle ("I've been feeling overwhelmed"), or a dream ("I've always wanted to start my own business, but I'm terrified").

• Step 3: Notice how it feels to be seen. Notice how they respond. Most likely, they'll appreciate your honesty and share something in return.

• Step 4: Reflect on the experience. How did vulnerability change your connection? How did it make you feel about yourself?

Start small, but start somewhere. Vulnerability is a muscle—the more you use it, the stronger it gets.

Final Words of This Chapter

Vulnerability is a risk worth taking. It's how we find the people who truly see us, and it's how we learn to see ourselves. Don't hide your heart—let it shine, flaws and all. The world doesn't need your perfection; it needs your truth. Be brave, be vulnerable, and watch how it transforms your life.

Chapter 33: The Healing Power of Nature

"Nature doesn't judge. It heals. Go to it when the world feels heavy."

— Jagat Sandhu

1. The World Beyond the Noise

In our fast-paced, technology-driven world, it's easy to feel overwhelmed. Notifications buzz, deadlines loom, and the constant noise of modern life can leave us feeling disconnected—from ourselves, from others, from the earth. But there's a place where the noise fades, where we can find peace and healing: nature. The sound of leaves rustling in the wind, the feel of grass under your feet, the sight of a sunset painting the sky—it all reminds us that we're part of something bigger, something timeless.

I've always found solace in nature, especially during difficult times. A few years ago, I went through a painful breakup. My heart felt shattered, and I couldn't escape the thoughts that swirled in my mind. I'd lie awake at night, replaying every moment, wondering what I could have done differently. One day, I couldn't take it anymore. I grabbed my shoes, turned off my phone, and drove to a nearby forest. I walked for hours, listening to the crunch of leaves under my feet, the chirping of birds, the gentle hum of a stream. For the first time in weeks, I felt calm. Nature didn't ask me to explain my pain—it simply held space for it.

2. A Story of Solace

That day in the forest reminded me of a story I heard from a friend named Meera. Meera had always been a city girl, thriving on the hustle and bustle of urban life. But when her mother passed away unexpectedly, she felt unmoored. The grief was overwhelming, and the city's noise only made it worse. She couldn't find peace in her apartment, surrounded by the constant hum of traffic and the pressure to "move on." On a whim, she decided to visit a national park a few hours away.

Meera spent a weekend camping alone—no phone, no distractions, just her and the wilderness. She hiked through dense forests, sat by a lake, and watched the stars at night. She told me, "For the first time since my mom died, I felt like I could breathe. The trees didn't judge me for crying. The water didn't rush me to heal. Nature just let me be." Over that weekend, Meera felt her grief soften. She didn't "get over" her loss, but she found a way to carry it. Nature became her sanctuary, a place where she could return whenever life felt too heavy.

3. Why Nature Heals

Nature heals because it operates on a different rhythm than our modern lives. It doesn't rush, yet everything gets done. A flower blooms when it's ready, not a moment sooner. A river flows at its own pace, carving its path over centuries. When we step into nature, we're reminded to slow down, to let go of the urgency that defines so much of our lives. We're reminded that we, too, are part of this natural rhythm—that we don't have to have it all figured out right now.

Science supports this. Studies have shown that spending time in nature reduces stress, lowers blood pressure, and improves mental health. The Japanese practice of shinrin-yoku, or "forest bathing," has been proven to boost mood and immune function simply by immersing oneself in a forest. But beyond the science, there's a deeper truth: nature heals because it accepts us as we are. It doesn't care about our failures, our insecurities, our to-do lists. It simply exists, and in its presence, we can exist too.

4. Religious Teachings on Nature

Across spiritual traditions, nature is revered as a sacred teacher, a reflection of the divine, and a source of healing.

Guru Granth Sahib Ji:

"Pavan guru paani pita, matadharatmahat."

(Air is the Guru, water the father, and earth the great mother.)

In Sikhism, nature is seen as a manifestation of God's creation. The air we breathe, the water we drink, the earth we walk on— they're all divine gifts, meant to guide and nurture us.

Quran:

"Do you not see that Allah sends down rain from the sky, and We produce thereby fruits of varying colors?"

— SurahFatir 35:27

The Quran often points to nature as a sign of God's mercy and wisdom. When we connect with the natural world, we connect with the Creator.

5. Nature as a Mirror

Nature doesn't just heal—it reflects. When you watch a tree bend in the wind but not break, you see resilience. When you see a flower bloom through a crack in the pavement, you see hope.

Nature mirrors the qualities we need to cultivate in ourselves: patience, strength, perseverance, beauty in imperfection.

I remember a time when I felt stuck in my writing. I was struggling with a chapter, second-guessing every word, feeling like I'd never finish this book. I took a break and went to a nearby beach. As I watched the waves crash against the shore, I noticed how they never stopped. They'd pull back, then come forward again, over and over, tirelessly shaping the sand. It hit me: progress doesn't have to be fast or perfect. It just has to be consistent. The waves didn't judge themselves for retreating—they just kept moving forward. That day, nature taught me to keep going, even when I felt like giving up.

6. A Nature Practice for Healing

Here's a simple practice to help you connect with nature's healing power:

• Step 1: Find a natural space near you—a park, a forest, a beach, even your backyard.

• Step 2: Spend at least 10 minutes there with no distractions. Leave your phone behind or turn it off.

• Step 3: Engage your senses. What do you see? The colors of the leaves, the movement of the clouds? What do you hear? The rustle of the wind, the chirping of birds? What do you feel? The ground beneath you, the air on your skin?

• Step 4: Take a deep breath and say a quiet thank you to nature for holding space for you. Let it remind you that you're enough, just as you are.

I do this practice whenever I feel overwhelmed, and it always helps. Nature has a way of putting things in perspective, of reminding me that my worries are small compared to the vastness of the world.

7. Making Nature a Part of Your Life

You don't need to live near a forest or a beach to experience nature's healing power. Even small doses can make a difference. Keep a plant on your desk and notice how it grows. Take a walk in your neighborhood and look for signs of nature—a tree, a flower, a bird. Open your window and let the fresh air in. Nature is everywhere, waiting to hold you, if you let it.

I've made it a habit to spend time in nature every week. Sometimes it's a hike, sometimes it's just sitting in my garden. But every time, I come back feeling lighter, clearer, more grounded. Nature has become my therapist, my teacher, my friend.

Final Words of This Chapter

Nature doesn't judge, doesn't rush, doesn't demand. It heals, simply by being. When the world feels heavy, step outside. Let the earth hold you, let the trees teach you, let the wind remind you that you're alive. Nature is waiting to heal you—are you ready to let it?

Chapter 34: The Gift of Forgiveness

"Forgiveness is not for them—it's for you. It's the key to your own freedom."

— Jagat Sandhu

1. The Weight of Resentment

Holding onto anger is like carrying a hot coal in your hand—you're the one who gets burned. Resentment festers, eating away at your peace, your joy, your ability to move forward. Forgiveness, on the other hand, is a gift you give yourself. It doesn't mean excusing what happened or pretending it didn't hurt. It means choosing peace over pain, freedom over bondage.

I've carried my share of resentment. A few years ago, a close friend betrayed my trust. We'd been inseparable, sharing everything—dreams, fears, secrets. But she started spreading rumors about me, things that weren't true, things that hurt my reputation and my heart. I was furious. I cut her out of my life, but I couldn't let go of the anger. Every time I thought of her, I'd feel my chest tighten, my stomach churn. I was holding onto that anger like a shield, thinking it protected me. But all it did was keep me stuck.

2. A Story of Letting Go

My cousin Arjun went through something similar. He had a falling out with a friend who borrowed money and never paid it back. Arjun felt betrayed, especially because he'd gone out of his way to help this friend during a tough time. For years, he carried that grudge. He'd see his friend's name on social media and feel a surge of bitterness. It affected his relationships—he became guarded, less trusting, always waiting for the next betrayal.

One day, Arjun decided he'd had enough. He didn't want to carry that weight anymore. He wrote a letter to his friend—not to send, but to release. In the letter, he poured out his anger, his hurt, his disappointment. Then he wrote, "I forgive you, not because you deserve it, but because I deserve peace." He burned the letter, letting the ashes symbolize the release of his resentment. Arjun told me that act changed him. He felt lighter, freer. He started smiling more, loving more. Forgiveness didn't erase the past, but it cleared the path for his future.

3. Why Forgiveness Feels So Hard

Forgiveness feels hard because it goes against our instincts. When someone hurts us, we want justice. We want them to feel the pain they caused us. We think holding onto anger gives us power, but it doesn't—it gives the other person power over us. As long as we're holding onto resentment, we're tied to the person who hurt us. We're letting them live rent-free in our minds, controlling our emotions, our peace.

I've seen this in my own life. With my friend who betrayed me, I thought my anger was a form of strength. I thought it showed I wasn't weak, that I wouldn't let her "win." But the longer I held onto that anger, the more I realized I was the one losing. I was losing sleep, losing joy, losing myself. Forgiveness felt like letting her off the hook, but in reality, it was letting myself off the hook. It was choosing my peace over my pride.

4. Religious Teachings on Forgiveness

Forgiveness is a central theme in many spiritual traditions. It's seen as a path to liberation, a way to free ourselves from the chains of anger and hurt.

Bible:

"Forgive, and you will be forgiven."

— Luke 6:37

This verse reminds us that forgiveness is a cycle—what we give, we receive. When we forgive others, we open ourselves to healing and grace.

Quran:

"The repayment of a bad action is one equivalent to it, but whoever pardons and makes reconciliation—his reward is with Allah."

— Surah Ash-Shura 42:40

The Quran teaches that forgiveness is a noble act, one that brings us closer to God. It's not about weakness—it's about strength.

5. The Difference Between Forgiveness and Reconciliation

It's important to understand that forgiveness doesn't mean reconciliation. You can forgive someone without inviting them back into your life. Forgiveness is about releasing the emotional hold they have on you; reconciliation is about rebuilding trust, which isn't always possible or healthy. For example, I forgave my friend who betrayed me, but I didn't reach out to her. I didn't feel safe with her anymore, and that's okay. Forgiveness is for your peace, not their comfort.

I've seen this distinction play out in others' lives too. A woman I met at a retreat, Sana, had been abused by her father as a child. She carried that pain for years, hating him, hating herself for not being able to let go. Through therapy, she learned to forgive—not because her father deserved it, but because she did. She didn't reconnect with him; she didn't need to. But she released the anger that was poisoning her. Forgiveness gave her the freedom to live again.

6. A Forgiveness Exercise

Here's an exercise to help you practice forgiveness:

• Step 1: Think of someone who hurt you. It could be a big betrayal or a small slight—whatever feels heavy.

• Step 2: Write down what they did and how it made you feel. Be honest, raw, unfiltered.

• Step 3: Write a forgiveness statement: "I forgive you, [name], not because you deserve it, but because I deserve peace."

• Step 4: Visualize releasing the hurt. Imagine it as a heavy stone you've been carrying—see yourself setting it down, walking away, feeling lighter.

• Step 5: Reflect on how you feel. You might need to repeat this process over time—forgiveness isn't always a one-time act.

I did this exercise with my friend's betrayal, and it was transformative. It didn't happen overnight, but slowly, I felt the anger loosen its grip. I felt free.

7. The Freedom of Forgiveness

Forgiveness is a journey, not a destination. Some days, you'll feel at peace; other days, the hurt might resurface. That's okay. The goal isn't to erase the past—it's to stop letting the past control your present. When you forgive, you take back your power. You say, "This hurt me, but it won't define me."

I think back to Arjun's story. After he forgave his friend, he didn't just let go of the grudge—he let go of the fear of being hurt again. He opened himself up to new friendships, to trust, to love. Forgiveness didn't change what happened, but it changed him. It gave him the freedom to live fully again.

Final Words of This Chapter

Forgiveness is a gift you give yourself. It doesn't mean what happened was okay—it means you're ready to move forward. Let go of the coal you've been carrying; your hands were meant to hold joy. Who do you need to forgive today? Start with them—or start with yourself. Either way, choose freedom.

Chapter 35: The Strength in Asking for Help

"Asking for help isn't weakness—it's a sign you're ready to grow."

1. The Myth of Doing It All Alone

We live in a culture that glorifies independence. We're taught that strength means doing it all alone, that asking for help makes us weak or needy. But this is a myth. Real strength isn't about carrying the world on your shoulders—it's about knowing when you need support and having the courage to ask for it. Asking for help doesn't make you less—it makes you more.

I used to believe the myth of independence. I thought I had to handle everything on my own—my struggles, my fears, my dreams. When I was in my early twenties, I went through a period of intense anxiety. My heart would race, my thoughts would spiral, and I felt like I was drowning. But I didn't tell anyone. I didn't want to burden my friends or family, didn't want them to see me as weak. So I kept it all inside, pretending I was fine, while inside, I was falling apart.

2. A Story of Support

One day, I couldn't pretend anymore. I was sitting with a close friend, trying to act normal, but I broke down. Through tears, I said, "I need help. I don't know what's wrong with me." I was terrified she'd judge me, but instead, she hugged me and said, "I'm so glad you told me. We'll figure this out together." That conversation was a turning point. My friend encouraged me to see a therapist, and over the next few months, I learned tools to manage my anxiety. I started journaling, practicing mindfulness, and talking openly about my struggles. Asking for help wasn't failure—it was my first step to healing.

I've seen this in others' lives too. A colleague of mine, Ravi, was struggling with burnout at work. He was working long hours, barely sleeping, and his health was deteriorating. But he didn't tell anyone—he thought he had to "man up" and handle it. One day, he collapsed from exhaustion and ended up in the hospital. That was his wake-up call. He told his boss, "I can't do this alone. I need support." To his surprise, his boss was understanding. They adjusted his workload, and Ravi started seeing a counselor. He told me, "I wish I'd asked for help sooner. I didn't realize how much I was carrying."

3. Why Asking for Help Feels So Hard

Asking for help feels hard because it challenges our ego. We want to be seen as capable, strong, in control. Admitting we need help feels like admitting we've failed. It's also tied to fear—fear of rejection, fear of judgment, fear of being a burden. We worry that if we ask for help, people will think less of us, or worse, they'll say no.

I've felt this fear myself. When I was struggling with anxiety, I worried that if I told my friends, they'd see me differently. I thought they'd think I was "too much" or that I was being dramatic. But the opposite happened—they respected me more for being honest. They appreciated that I trusted them enough to share my truth. Asking for help didn't push them away—it brought us closer.

4. The Wisdom of Interdependence

Oprah Winfrey once said:

"You don't have to do it alone. We rise by lifting others—and letting others lift us."

This idea of interdependence is powerful. We're not meant to go through life alone. We're meant to support each other, to lean on each other, to grow together. Asking for help isn't a sign of weakness—it's a sign of wisdom. It's recognizing that we're all human, that we all have limits, that we all need each other.

I've seen this in my community. During the pandemic, a neighbor of mine, Mrs. Kapoor, lost her husband. She was grieving, but she didn't know how to ask for help. One day, she broke down in front of me, saying, "I don't know how to do this alone." I rallied our neighbors—we started bringing her meals, checking in on her, helping with errands. Mrs. Kapoor told me later, "I was so scared to ask, but your help saved me." Her vulnerability allowed us to show up for her, and it strengthened our community.

5. Religious Teachings on Community

Many spiritual traditions emphasize the importance of community and mutual support. We're reminded that we're stronger together than we are apart.

Bible:

"Bear one another's burdens, and so fulfill the law of Christ."

— Galatians 6:2

This verse teaches that helping each other is a sacred act. When we ask for help, we give others the chance to live out this principle.

Guru Granth Sahib Ji:

"Sangatvich sukh hai, sangatvich shanti hai."

(In the company of the holy, there is peace and happiness.)

Sikhism teaches that community is a source of strength. When we lean on others, we find peace.

6. A Help-Seeking Challenge

Here's a challenge to help you practice asking for help:

• Step 1: Think of one area where you're struggling right now. It could be something practical (like needing help with a project) or emotional (like needing someone to talk to).

• Step 2: Identify someone you trust—a friend, a family member, a professional.

• Step 3: Reach out to them and be honest. Say, "I need help with this. Can you support me?" Be specific about what you need.

• Step 4: Notice how it feels to receive help. Notice how it changes your load, your perspective, your connection with that person.

I did this challenge recently. I was feeling overwhelmed with a deadline and asked a friend to help me brainstorm ideas. Not only did we come up with great solutions, but I felt so supported. Asking for help reminded me that I don't have to do it all alone.

7. The Strength in Vulnerability

Asking for help is an act of vulnerability, and as we learned in Chapter 32, vulnerability is the birthplace of connection. When you ask for help, you're saying, "I trust you with my struggle." That trust deepens your relationships. It also shows others that it's okay to need support, that it's okay to be human.

I think back to Ravi's story. After he asked for help at work, he started being more open with his team. He'd admit when he was struggling, and they'd admit their struggles too. It created a culture of honesty and support. Asking for help didn't make Ravi weaker—it made his team stronger.

Final Words of This Chapter

You weren't meant to carry the world alone. Asking for help is a bridge, not a burden. It's a sign of strength, a step toward growth, a way to deepen your connections. Let others lift you—you deserve it. Who can you ask for help today?

Chapter 36: The Beauty of Imperfection

"Perfection is a myth. Your flaws are what make you real—and real is beautiful."

— Jagat Sandhu

1. The Pressure to Be Perfect

We live in a world that glorifies perfection. Social media shows us curated lives—perfect bodies, perfect homes, perfect careers. Advertisements tell us we need to look a certain way, act a certain way, be a certain way to be worthy. But perfection is a myth. It's a moving target you'll never hit, a standard that keeps changing, a lie that keeps us trapped in self-doubt.

I've felt this pressure my whole life. Growing up, I was a straight-A student, always striving to be the best. I thought perfection would make me lovable, worthy, enough. But no matter how hard I tried, I never felt like I measured up. I'd get a 98 on a test and beat myself up over the 2 points I missed. I'd compare myself to my classmates, my cousins, even strangers on the internet. Perfection became my prison, and I didn't even realize it.

2. A Story of Acceptance

My friend Sonia helped me see perfection in a new light. Sonia had scars on her arms from a childhood accident. For years, she hid them, wearing long sleeves even in the summer, ashamed of her "imperfection." She thought her scars made her ugly, that people would judge her if they saw them. But one day, at a family party, she decided to wear a short-sleeved dress. Her scars were visible, and she was nervous.

During the party, a little girl—her niece—came up to her and said, "Auntie, your scars look like stars!" Sonia was stunned. She'd spent years hating her scars, but this child saw them as beautiful. That moment shifted something in Sonia. She started seeing her scars as stories, not flaws. They were proof of her survival, her strength, her journey. Sonia stopped hiding them, and over time, she stopped hiding herself. Her story taught me that our imperfections don't make us less—they make us human.

3. Why We Chase Perfection

We chase perfection because we think it's the key to love, success, happiness. We think, "If I'm perfect, I'll be enough." But this belief is rooted in fear—fear of rejection, fear of failure, fear of not being loved. The irony is, the more we chase perfection, the more we disconnect from ourselves. We become so focused on fixing our flaws that we forget to celebrate our strengths.

I've seen this in my own life and in others'. A friend of mine, Priyanka, was obsessed with her appearance. She'd spend hours on her makeup, always trying to look "flawless." But she was never happy with how she looked. She'd point out every perceived imperfection—her nose was too big, her skin wasn't clear enough, her smile wasn't perfect. I told her, "You're beautiful just as you are," but she couldn't hear it. The pursuit of perfection blinded her to her own beauty.

4. Religious Teachings on Acceptance

Spiritual traditions remind us that we're not meant to be perfect— we're meant to be real. Our flaws are part of our humanity, part of our journey to growth and connection.

Bhagavad Gita:

"The wise see the same in all—whether perfect or flawed."

— Chapter 5, Verse 18

This verse teaches that true wisdom lies in accepting ourselves and others as we are, not as we think we should be. God doesn't demand perfection—God demands authenticity.

Guru Granth Sahib Ji:

"Sabhkichh tera, tera hai, Nanak."

(Everything is Yours, everything belongs to You, O Nanak.)

This teaching reminds us that we are God's creation, flaws and all. Our imperfections are part of the divine design.

5. The Beauty of Being Real

Imperfection is what makes us real, relatable, lovable. Think about the people you admire most. Do you love them because they're perfect, or because they're human? I bet it's the latter. We're drawn to people who are authentic, who show their scars, who laugh at their mistakes, who let us see their true selves.

I've learned this in my own relationships. My best friend, Anjali, is someone I admire not because she's perfect, but because she's real. She's clumsy, she's forgetful, she's a mess sometimes—but she's also kind, funny, and fiercely loyal. Her imperfections make her who she is, and I wouldn't change a thing about her. Seeing her embrace her flaws helped me embrace mine. I started letting go of the need to be perfect and focused on being present, being me.

6. An Imperfection Practice

Here's a practice to help you embrace your imperfections:

• Step 1: Look in the mirror and name three things you've criticized about yourself. It could be physical (like your weight) or emotional (like your anxiety).

• Step 2: For each one, say, "I love you anyway." For example, "I've criticized my body for not being thin enough, but I love you anyway."

• Step 3: Write down three things you love about yourself—things that have nothing to do with perfection. Maybe you love your sense of humor, your compassion, your curiosity.

• Step 4: Reflect on how it feels to accept yourself as you are. Notice the shift from judgment to love.

I did this practice recently, and it was eye-opening. I realized how much energy I'd been wasting on self-criticism, and how much freer I felt when I let that go.

7. Imperfection as a Path to Growth

Imperfection isn't something to fix—it's something to celebrate. Your flaws are part of your story, part of what makes you unique. They're also a path to growth. When you embrace your imperfections, you give yourself permission to learn, to mess up, to try again. You stop striving for an impossible standard and start striving for a meaningful life.

I think back to Sonia's story. Her scars weren't just physical—they were emotional too. By accepting them, she learned to accept herself. She became more confident, more open, more connected to others. Her imperfection didn't hold her back—it propelled her forward.

Final Words of This Chapter

You are not a project to be fixed. You are a story to be lived—messy, imperfect, and beautiful. Your flaws don't define your worth—they define your humanity. Embrace them, love them, let them teach you. The world doesn't need your perfection; it needs your realness. Be beautifully, wonderfully, imperfectly you.

Chapter 37: The Power of Small Wins

"Big victories are built on small wins—celebrate every step, no matter how small."

1. The Overlooked Victories

We live in a world that celebrates big victories—graduations, promotions, weddings, major milestones. But what about the small wins? The ones that don't get applause, that don't make it to social media, that no one else sees? Getting out of bed on a hard day, finishing a task you've been dreading, choosing to be kind when you're angry—these are victories too, and they matter just as much as the big ones.

I've learned to appreciate small wins through my own struggles. When I was writing this book, there were days when I felt completely stuck. I'd stare at a blank page, overwhelmed by the enormity of the project. On those days, writing a single sentence felt impossible. But I started setting small goals: write for 10 minutes, finish one paragraph, come up with one idea. Some days, that's all I could do. But those small wins added up. A sentence became a paragraph, a paragraph became a page, and eventually, a page became a chapter. I realized that big victories are just a collection of small ones.

2. A Story of Incremental Progress

Let me tell you about my friend Sameer, who taught me the power of small wins. Sameer had always struggled with his weight. He'd tried every diet, every workout plan, but nothing stuck. He'd lose a few pounds, then gain them back, feeling like a failure. He told me,

"I just want to be healthy, but it feels impossible." I suggested he focus on small, manageable goals instead of trying to overhaul his life overnight.

Sameer started with one small win: drinking a glass of water first thing in the morning. That was it—no big changes, just one glass of water. After a week, he added another small win: walking for 10 minutes a day. Over time, he built on these habits—eating one vegetable with every meal, taking the stairs instead of the elevator, stretching for 5 minutes before bed. He didn't transform his life overnight, but over the course of a year, he lost 30 pounds. More importantly, he felt stronger, happier, more in control. Sameer's story showed me that small wins aren't just steps toward a goal—they're proof that you're capable of change.

3. Why Small Wins Matter

Small wins matter because they build momentum. When you achieve something small, you prove to yourself that you can do hard things. That sense of accomplishment, no matter how tiny, boosts your confidence and motivates you to keep going. It's like rolling a snowball down a hill—each small win makes the snowball bigger, stronger, unstoppable.

Science supports this. Research in psychology shows that small wins trigger the release of dopamine, the "feel-good" chemical in your brain. This creates a positive feedback loop: you achieve something small, you feel good, and you're more likely to take on the next challenge. I've seen this in my own life. On days when I feel overwhelmed, I focus on one small task—like answering an email or organizing my desk. Completing that task gives me a sense of control, and I'm more likely to tackle the next thing on my list.

4. Religious Teachings on Patience

Many spiritual traditions emphasize the importance of patience and small steps on the path to growth. Big changes don't happen overnight—they happen through consistent, faithful effort.

Bhagavad Gita:

"Little by little, through patience and repeated effort, the mind can be controlled."

— Chapter 6, Verse 25

This verse reminds us that progress is a gradual process. Small, consistent actions lead to lasting change.

Quran:

"Indeed, those who have believed and done righteous deeds—the Most Merciful will appoint for them affection."

— Surah Maryam 19:96

The Quran teaches that good deeds, no matter how small, are rewarded. Every small win in the direction of righteousness brings you closer to peace.

5. Celebrating the Unseen Wins

Some of the most important small wins are the ones no one else sees. Getting out of bed when you're depressed, choosing not to lash out when you're angry, taking a deep breath instead of panicking—these are victories, even if they don't come with applause. They're proof of your resilience, your growth, your strength.

I remember a day when I was grieving the loss of my friend. I didn't want to do anything—I just wanted to stay in bed, shut the world out. But I told myself, "Just get up and make your bed." That was my small win for the day. It didn't seem like much, but it gave me a sense of control, a reason to keep going. Over time, those small wins—making my bed, taking a shower, going for a walk—helped me through my grief. They reminded me that healing happens in small steps.

6. A Small Wins Practice

Here's a practice to help you celebrate small wins:

• Step 1: At the start of each day, set one small, achievable goal. It could be drinking a glass of water, writing for 10 minutes, or texting a friend to check in.

• Step 2: When you complete that goal, celebrate it. Say to yourself, "I did it. I'm proud of myself." Maybe even write it down in a journal.

• Step 3: Reflect on how that small win made you feel. Did it give you a sense of accomplishment? Did it motivate you to do more?

• Step 4: Build on it. Add another small goal the next day, and keep going.

I've been doing this practice for a while, and it's changed how I approach my goals. Instead of feeling overwhelmed by the big picture, I focus on the next small step. It's made me more consistent, more confident, more compassionate with myself.

7. The Compound Effect of Small Wins

Small wins have a compound effect. Each one builds on the last, creating a foundation for bigger victories. Think of Sameer's story—his glass of water led to a 10-minute walk, which led to healthier eating, which led to a 30-pound weight loss. Or my own journey with this book—a sentence became a paragraph, a paragraph became a chapter, and now, here we are.

The beauty of small wins is that they're accessible to everyone. You don't need talent, money, or resources to achieve them. You just need intention, consistency, and a willingness to celebrate yourself. Every small win is a reminder that you're moving forward, even if the progress feels slow.

Final Words of This Chapter

Big victories are built on small wins. Don't wait for the finish line to celebrate—honor every step, every effort, every moment of courage. You're doing better than you think, and every small win is proof of that. What's one small win you can celebrate today?

Chapter 38: The Gift of Curiosity

"Curiosity is the spark that lights the fire of growth. Stay curious, and you'll never stop growing."

— Jagat Sandhu

1. The Childlike Wonder We Lose

When we were children, curiosity was our default state. We'd ask endless questions—Why is the sky blue? How do birds fly? What happens if I mix these colors? We explored the world with wide eyes, eager to learn, unafraid of not knowing. But as we grow older, we often lose that sense of wonder. We stop asking questions, stop exploring, stop seeking. We settle into routines, into what's comfortable, into what we already know.

I remember being a curious child. I'd spend hours in my backyard, digging in the dirt, looking for bugs, imagining they were part of a secret world. I'd ask my parents a million questions, driving them crazy with my "whys" and "hows." But as I got older, I stopped asking. I started caring more about fitting in, about getting good grades, about being "successful." Curiosity felt like a luxury I couldn't afford. It wasn't until I rediscovered it as an adult that I realized how much I'd been missing.

2. A Story of Rediscovery

Let me tell you about my friend Ayesha, who reignited her curiosity later in life. Ayesha was a software engineer, good at her job but unfulfilled. She'd always been practical, focused on stability over passion. But one day, she stumbled upon a documentary about marine biology. She was fascinated by the underwater world—the colors of the coral reefs, the strange creatures of the deep. It awakened something in her, a curiosity she hadn't felt since childhood.

Ayesha started reading books about the ocean, watching more documentaries, even taking an online course. On a whim, she signed up for a scuba diving trip. She told me, "I was terrified, but I had to see it for myself." Under the water, she found a world more beautiful than she'd ever imagined. That experience changed her. She didn't quit her job, but she started volunteering with a marine conservation group on weekends. Curiosity didn't just give her a hobby—it gave her a purpose. Ayesha's story reminded me that curiosity can lead us to places we never expected.

3. Why Curiosity Matters

Curiosity is the spark that lights the fire of growth. It's what drives us to learn, to explore, to create. When we're curious, we're open to new ideas, new experiences, new perspectives. We're willing to step outside our comfort zones, to take risks, to fail and try again. Curiosity keeps us young, keeps us engaged,

Chapter 38: The Gift of Curiosity (Continued)

"Curiosity is the spark that lights the fire of growth. Stay curious, and you'll never stop growing."

— Jagat Sandhu

6. A Curiosity Practice (Continued)

passion that brought me so much joy. I started noticing details I'd never seen before—the way sunlight filters through leaves, the texture of a flower petal, the expression on a stranger's face. Curiosity didn't just teach me a skill; it taught me to see the world with fresh eyes.

7. Curiosity as a Lifelong Companion

Curiosity isn't a one-time act—it's a lifelong companion. It's what keeps you growing, evolving, discovering. The most fulfilled people I know are the ones who never stop being curious. They read, they travel, they ask questions, they try new things. They approach life with a sense of wonder, even in the face of challenges.

I think back to Ayesha's story. Her curiosity about marine biology didn't just lead her to scuba diving—it led her to a deeper purpose. She started advocating for ocean conservation, speaking at local events, and inspiring others to care about the planet. Her curiosity didn't just change her life; it changed the lives of those around her. That's the power of staying curious—it doesn't just light your fire; it lights the world.

Curiosity also helps us navigate life's uncertainties. When we're curious, we're less afraid of the unknown because we see it as an opportunity to learn. I've found this to be true in my own journey. When I started writing this book, I was terrified of failing. But instead of letting fear stop me, I got curious. I asked, "What can I learn from this process? What can I discover about myself?" That curiosity turned my fear into fuel. It helped me keep going, even when the road felt hard.

8. Overcoming the Barriers to Curiosity

Sometimes, curiosity gets stifled by fear, busyness, or complacency. We're afraid of looking foolish, so we stop asking questions. We're too busy to explore, so we stick to what we know. We get comfortable, so we stop seeking. But curiosity is worth fighting for. It's worth the risk, the time, the effort.

I've had to push past my own barriers to curiosity. A few years ago, I wanted to learn how to cook traditional Punjabi dishes, but I was intimidated. I'd never been great in the kitchen, and I worried I'd mess up. But I decided to lean into my curiosity. I asked my mom for recipes, watched cooking videos, and experimented with spices. I burned a few dishes, but I also created some meals I was proud of. Curiosity helped me overcome my fear of failure—it reminded me that learning is a process, not a performance.

If you feel stuck, ask yourself: What's holding me back from being curious? Is it fear? Busyness? A belief that you already know enough? Whatever it is, challenge it. Give yourself permission to be a beginner, to ask questions, to explore. Curiosity isn't about having all the answers—it's about loving the questions.

Final Words of This Chapter

Curiosity is a gift you can give yourself every day. It's the spark that lights the fire of growth, the key that unlocks new doors, the lens that reveals the beauty of the world. Stay curious, and you'll never stop growing. What are you curious about today? Follow that spark—it might just lead you to a life more vibrant than you ever imagined.

Chapter 39: The Strength of Stillness

"In the stillness, you'll find the answers you've been searching for."

— Jagat Sandhu

1. The Noise of Modern Life

We live in a world that never stops moving. Our days are filled with noise—emails, notifications, meetings, deadlines, the constant hum of a busy life. We're always doing, always rushing, always chasing the next thing. But in all that noise, we lose something precious: stillness. Stillness is the space where we can hear ourselves think, feel our hearts beat, connect with our deepest truths.

I used to be addicted to busyness. I thought productivity was the measure of my worth—if I wasn't doing something, I was wasting time. I'd fill my days with tasks, even when I was exhausted, because stillness felt uncomfortable. It forced me to face things I didn't want to face—my fears, my doubts, my unhealed wounds. But over time, I realized that running from stillness was also running from myself. It wasn't until I embraced it that I found the clarity I'd been searching for.

2. A Story of Finding Peace

Let me tell you about my friend Karan, who discovered the power of stillness during a difficult time. Karan was a high-powered executive, always on the go, managing a team of 50 people. He thrived on the chaos of his job, but it came at a cost. He was stressed, irritable, and disconnected from his family. One day, he had a panic attack at work—his heart raced, his chest tightened, and he thought he was having a heart attack. It was a wake-up call.

Karan's doctor told him he needed to slow down, so he started practicing meditation. At first, he hated it. Sitting still for 10 minutes felt like torture—he'd fidget, check his phone, make excuses to get up. But he kept at it, and slowly, he started to notice a change. In the stillness, he could hear his own thoughts, feel his own emotions. He realized how much he'd been neglecting his well-being, how much he missed his kids' laughter, how much he needed to reconnect with himself. Stillness became his sanctuary. Karan told me, "I used to think I didn't have time to stop. But now I know I can't afford not to."

3. Why Stillness Feels Uncomfortable

Stillness feels uncomfortable because it strips away the distractions we use to avoid ourselves. When we're busy, we don't have to face our fears, our pain, our unanswered questions. But in stillness, there's nowhere to hide. We're forced to sit with our thoughts, our feelings, our truths—and that can be scary.

I've felt this discomfort myself. The first time I tried meditation, I lasted about 30 seconds before I gave up. My mind was racing with to-do lists, worries, random thoughts. I thought, "This isn't for me." But I kept trying, and over time, I learned to sit with the discomfort. I learned that the thoughts racing through my mind weren't the enemy—they were messengers, telling me what I needed to address. Stillness didn't make me anxious; it showed me where my anxiety was coming from.

4. Religious Teachings on Stillness

Stillness is a sacred practice in many spiritual traditions. It's seen as a way to connect with the divine, to find peace, to hear the whispers of truth.

Bible:

"Be still, and know that I am God."

— Psalm 46:10

This verse reminds us that in stillness, we can feel God's presence. When we quiet the noise of the world, we make space for the divine to speak.

Bhagavad Gita:

"When the mind is still, the self is revealed."

— Chapter 6, Verse 20

The Gita teaches that stillness is the path to self-realization. When we quiet our minds, we discover who we truly are.

5. The Benefits of Stillness

Stillness has profound benefits. It reduces stress, improves focus, and helps us process our emotions. But more than that, it connects us to our inner wisdom. In the stillness, we can hear the answers we've been searching for—answers about our purpose, our relationships, our next steps.

I've experienced this in my own life. A few months ago, I was struggling with a big decision—whether to take a new job opportunity or stay focused on writing. I was torn, and no amount of pros-and-cons lists helped. So I decided to sit in stillness. I turned off my phone, sat on my balcony, and just breathed. At first, my mind was loud, but slowly, it quieted. And in that quiet, I heard a small voice say, "Follow your heart." I knew what I needed to do—I turned down the job and kept writing. Stillness gave me the clarity I couldn't find in the noise.

6. A Stillness Practice

Here's a simple practice to help you embrace stillness:

• Step 1: Find a quiet space where you won't be disturbed. It could be a corner of your home, a park, or even your car.

• Step 2: Sit comfortably and close your eyes. Take a few deep breaths, noticing the air moving in and out.

• Step 3: For 5 minutes, just be. Don't try to stop your thoughts—let them come and go, like clouds passing in the sky. If you get distracted, gently bring your focus back to your breath.

• Step 4: After 5 minutes, reflect on how you feel. Do you feel calmer? Clearer? Did any insights come up?

I do this practice every morning, and it's become a sacred part of my day. It's not always easy—some days my mind is louder than others—but it always helps me start the day with intention.

7. Making Stillness a Habit

Stillness doesn't have to be a big production. You can find it in small moments—sitting quietly with your morning coffee, taking a deep breath before a meeting, pausing to watch the sunset. The key is to make it a habit, to weave it into your life like a thread of peace.

I've seen the difference this makes. Karan, the executive I mentioned earlier, now meditates for 10 minutes every day. He's calmer, more present, more connected to his family. He told me, "Stillness isn't just a break—it's a reset. It helps me show up as the person I want to be." His story reminds us that stillness isn't a luxury—it's a necessity.

8. The Answers in the Quiet

Stillness is where we find the answers we've been searching for. It's where we hear the whispers of our intuition, the guidance of our higher power, the truth of our hearts. The world is noisy, but your soul speaks in whispers. If you want to hear it, you have to get quiet.

I think back to that decision about my job. In the stillness, I didn't just find an answer—I found trust. I trusted myself, my path, my purpose. Stillness didn't just give me clarity; it gave me courage.

Final Words of This Chapter

In the stillness, you'll find the answers you've been searching for. Don't run from the quiet—embrace it. Let it hold you, guide you, heal you. The noise of the world will always be there, but so will the stillness, waiting to bring you back to yourself. Take a moment today to be still—what do you hear?

Chapter 40: The Power of Connection

"We are not islands—we are threads in a tapestry, woven together by connection."

— Jagat Sandhu

1. The Human Need for Connection

We are wired for connection. From the moment we're born, we seek it—through a mother's touch, a friend's laughter, a partner's embrace. Connection is what makes us human, what gives our lives meaning, what reminds us we're not alone. But in a world that's more connected than ever—through technology, social media, instant messaging—we often feel more isolated than ever.

I've felt this isolation myself. A few years ago, I moved to a new city for work. I didn't know anyone, and for the first time in my life, I felt truly alone. I had hundreds of "friends" on social media, but no one to call when I needed a real conversation. I'd scroll through my feed, seeing pictures of people laughing, traveling, living their best lives, and I'd feel even worse. It wasn't until I started building real connections—joining a book club, talking to my neighbors, calling old friends—that I felt like myself again. Technology can connect us on the surface, but true connection happens heart to heart.

2. A Story of Belonging

Let me tell you about Priyanka, a woman I met at that book club. Priyanka had grown up feeling like an outsider. She was shy, introverted, and struggled to make friends. As an adult, she threw herself into her career, thinking that success would fill the void.

But it didn't. She told me, "I had a great job, a nice apartment, but I felt so empty. I didn't have anyone to share it with."

Priyanka decided to step out of her comfort zone and join our book club. At first, she was quiet, nervous about speaking up. But over time, she started sharing—her thoughts on the books, her experiences, her dreams. The group welcomed her with open arms. We'd laugh together, debate together, sometimes cry together. Priyanka told me, "For the first time, I felt like I belonged. I realized I didn't need to be perfect to be loved—I just needed to be me." Connection gave Priyanka a sense of belonging she'd never had before, and it changed her life.

3. Why Connection Matters

Connection matters because it's the foundation of our well-being. Studies show that strong social connections improve mental health, reduce stress, and even increase longevity. People with close relationships are happier, healthier, and more resilient. But beyond the science, connection matters because it reminds us of our shared humanity. It reminds us that we're not alone in our struggles, our joys, our dreams.

I've seen this in my own life. During a tough period after my breakup, I felt like no one could understand my pain. But when I opened up to my friends, I found that many of them had been through similar heartaches. They shared their stories, their lessons, their hope. Those conversations didn't erase my pain, but they made it bearable. Connection reminded me that I wasn't alone—that we're all in this together.

4. Religious Teachings on Community

Many spiritual traditions emphasize the importance of community and connection. They remind us that we're stronger together, that we're meant to support each other, to love each other.

Guru Granth Sahib Ji:

"Sangatvich sukh hai, sangatvich shanti hai."

(In the company of the holy, there is peace and happiness.)

Sikhism teaches that connection with others—especially those who share your values—brings peace and joy.

Bible:

"For where two or three gather in my name, there am I with them."

— Matthew 18:20

This verse reminds us that connection is sacred. When we come together with love and intention, we invite the divine into our midst.

5. The Barriers to Connection

Sometimes, connection feels hard because of the barriers we put up. We're afraid of being vulnerable, afraid of rejection, afraid of not being enough. We hide behind screens, behind small talk, behind the fear of being truly seen. But real connection requires us to show up as we are—messy, imperfect, human.

I've struggled with this myself. When I moved to that new city, I was hesitant to reach out. I worried that people wouldn't like me, that I'd be too much or not enough. But I realized that connection starts with a single step—a hello, a smile, a question. When I joined that book club, I didn't know anyone, but I showed up anyway. I was nervous, but I shared anyway. And slowly, those small acts of courage led to real friendships. Connection isn't about being perfect—it's about being present.

6. A Connection Practice

Here's a practice to help you build deeper connections:

• Step 1: Think of someone you'd like to connect with more deeply—a friend, a family member, a colleague.

• Step 2: Reach out to them with intention. Invite them for a coffee, a walk, or a phone call. Say, "I'd love to catch up and really hear how you're doing."

• Step 3: During your time together, practice active listening. Put away your phone, make eye contact, ask questions, and really hear their story.

• Step 4: Share something real about yourself. It could be a joy, a struggle, a dream. Let them see the real you.

• Step 5: Reflect on how it felt to connect. Did it deepen your relationship? Did it make you feel more seen?

I did this practice with my sister recently. We've always been close, but life gets busy, and we don't always make time for deep conversations. I invited her for a walk, and we talked—really talked—about our hopes, our fears, our dreams. I learned things about her I didn't know, and I felt so much closer to her. Connection doesn't have to be complicated—it just has to be real.

7. Connection in Small Moments

You don't need grand gestures to build connection. Sometimes, it's the small moments that matter most—a kind word to a stranger, a smile to a neighbor, a thank-you to a coworker. These moments weave the threads of connection, creating a tapestry of belonging that holds us all.

I've made it a habit to connect in small ways every day. I'll chat with the cashier at the grocery store, ask my neighbor how their day was, send a quick text to a friend. These small acts don't take much time, but they make a big difference. They remind me—and others—that we're all part of the same human family.

8. The Ripple Effect of Connection

Connection has a ripple effect. When you connect with someone, you lift their spirits, and they're more likely to lift someone else's. It's a chain reaction of love, kindness, and belonging. I think back to Priyanka's story. Her decision to join our book club didn't just give her a sense of belonging—it gave all of us a new friend. Her presence made our group richer, warmer, more connected. One act of courage rippled out to touch us all.

Final Words of This Chapter

We are not islands—we are threads in a tapestry, woven together by connection. Don't let fear or busyness keep you from reaching out. Show up, be real, let others see you. The connections you build will remind you that you're never alone. Who can you connect with today?

Chapter 41: The Courage to Dream Big

"Your dreams are the whispers of your soul—dare to listen, dare to follow."

— Jagat Sandhu

1. The Dreams We Bury

We all have dreams—those big, wild, beautiful visions of what we want our lives to be. Maybe you dream of starting your own business, writing a book, traveling the world, or making a difference in your community. But too often, we bury those dreams. We tell ourselves they're unrealistic, that we're not good enough, that it's too late. We let fear, doubt, and practicality silence the whispers of our soul.

I buried my own dreams for years. When I was a child, I dreamed of being a writer. I'd spend hours scribbling stories, imagining my name on the cover of a book. But as I grew older, I started to doubt myself. I'd hear things like, "Writing isn't a real career," or "You'll never make money doing that." I let those voices drown out my dream, and I pursued a "safer" path instead. It wasn't until I was in my late twenties that I realized I couldn't keep ignoring my dream—it was a part of me, and it wasn't going away.

2. A Story of Daring to Dream

Let me tell you about my friend Rohan, who dared to dream big despite the odds. Rohan grew up in a small village where most people became farmers or laborers. But he had a different dream— he wanted to be a pilot. Everyone told him it was impossible. "People like us don't fly planes," his father said. "Focus on something practical." But Rohan couldn't let go of his dream. He'd watch planes fly overhead and imagine himself in the cockpit, soaring above the world.

Rohan worked odd jobs to save money, studied hard despite limited resources, and applied for scholarships. It took years of persistence, but he eventually got accepted into a flight school. When he earned his pilot's license, he became the first person from his village to fly a plane. He told me, "I didn't just achieve my dream—I showed others that they can dream too." Rohan's story taught me that big dreams require big courage, but they also create big change—for ourselves and for those around us.

3. Why We Fear Big Dreams

We fear big dreams because they come with big risks. What if we fail? What if we're not good enough? What if people laugh at us? These fears are real, but they're also illusions. They're stories we tell ourselves to stay safe, to stay small. The truth is, the biggest risk isn't failing—it's never trying. It's living a life that's less than what you're capable of, less than what you dream of.

I've felt this fear myself. When I decided to write this book, I was terrified. I worried I didn't have enough experience, that no one would read it, that I'd embarrass myself. But I realized that the fear of failure was nothing compared to the regret of not trying. I'd rather fail at something I love than succeed at something I don't. So I took the leap, and I'm so glad I did.

4. Religious Teachings on Faith and Vision

Spiritual traditions remind us that dreams are often a reflection of our divine purpose. They encourage us to have faith, to trust the path, to believe in the impossible.

Quran:

"And when you have decided, then rely upon Allah. Indeed, Allah loves those who rely upon Him."

— Surah Al-Imran 3:159

This verse teaches that when we pursue our dreams with faith, we're supported by a higher power. Trust the journey, even when it feels uncertain.

Bhagavad Gita:

"Set thy heart upon thy work, but never on its reward."

— Chapter 2, Verse 47

The Gita reminds us to focus on the effort, not the outcome. Pursue your dreams with dedication, and let the results unfold as they will.

5. The Power of Small Steps Toward Big Dreams

Big dreams can feel overwhelming, but they don't have to be. They're achieved through small, consistent steps. When I started writing this book, I didn't try to write it all at once. I set small goals—write for 30 minutes a day, finish one chapter a month. Those small steps added up, and now, here we are. Big dreams don't require big leaps—they require steady progress.

Rohan's journey was the same. He didn't become a pilot overnight. He took small steps—saving money, studying, applying for scholarships. Each step brought him closer to his dream, even when the path felt long. Small steps build momentum, and momentum builds miracles.

6. A Dreaming Practice

Here's a practice to help you reconnect with your big dreams:

• Step 1: Find a quiet space and close your eyes. Imagine your ideal life—what does it look like? What are you doing? Who are you with? Don't hold back—let yourself dream big.

• Step 2: Write down your dream in detail. Be specific. For example, "I want to start a nonprofit that helps children in need."

• Step 3: Identify one small step you can take toward that dream this week. Maybe it's researching nonprofits, taking a course, or talking to someone who's done it.

• Step 4: Take that step, and celebrate yourself for starting. Reflect on how it feels to move toward your dream.

I did this practice when I started writing. My dream was to finish this book, and my first small step was to write one page. That page became a chapter, and that chapter became this book. Small steps can lead to big dreams.

7. The Ripple Effect of Dreaming Big

When you dare to dream big, you don't just change your life—you inspire others to dream too. Rohan's story didn't just end with him becoming a pilot. His success inspired other kids in his village to dream bigger, to believe in themselves, to reach for more. One person's courage can spark a movement.

I've seen this in my own life. When I started writing, I shared my journey with friends. One of them, inspired by my courage, decided to pursue her dream of opening a bakery. She told me, "Seeing you go for your dream made me believe I could go for mine." Our dreams don't just belong to us—they belong to the world.

8. Dreaming Through the Doubts

There will always be doubts, always be naysayers, always be obstacles. But your dreams are worth fighting for. They're the whispers of your soul, guiding you toward your purpose. Don't let fear silence them. Don't let practicality bury them. Dream big, start small, keep going.

I think back to my own journey. Writing this book wasn't easy—there were days I wanted to give up, days I doubted myself. But every time I thought of quitting, I'd hear a small voice say, "This is your dream. Keep going." That voice, that dream, carried me through. It can carry you too.

Final Words of This Chapter

Your dreams are the whispers of your soul—dare to listen, dare to follow. They might scare you, they might challenge you, but they'll also lead you to a life that's truly yours. Don't bury your dreams—let them soar. What's the biggest dream you've been afraid to chase? Start today, with one small step.

Chapter 42: The Healing Power of Creativity

"Creativity is the language of your soul—speak it, and you'll find healing."

— Jagat Sandhu

1. The Universal Language of Creativity

Creativity is a universal language, one that transcends words, cultures, and boundaries. It's the way we express what's deepest within us—our joys, our pains, our hopes, our dreams. Whether it's painting, writing, dancing, cooking, or gardening, creativity allows us to speak the language of our soul. And in that expression, we find healing.

I've always found solace in creativity. When I was a teenager, I went through a rough patch—I felt lost, disconnected, unsure of who I was. I started writing poetry as a way to process my emotions. I'd sit in my room, pouring my heart onto the page, letting the words say what I couldn't. Those poems weren't masterpieces, but they were medicine. They helped me make sense of my feelings, helped me feel seen, helped me heal.

2. A Story of Creative Healing

Let me tell you about my friend Meera, who found healing through creativity. Meera had always loved to dance, but as an adult, she stopped. Life got in the way—work, family, responsibilities. When her mother passed away, Meera fell into a deep depression. She felt numb, unable to process her grief. Therapy helped, but she still felt stuck.

One day, Meera heard music playing at a community center. It was a dance class, and on a whim, she joined. As she moved to the rhythm, something shifted. She felt her grief rise to the surface, but this time, it didn't overwhelm her—it flowed through her. She danced through her tears, her anger, her longing. Over the next few months, Meera kept dancing. She told me, "Dance became my therapy. It gave me a way to feel my pain without being consumed by it." Creativity didn't erase Meera's grief, but it gave her a way to carry it.

3. Why Creativity Heals

Creativity heals because it allows us to externalize what's inside us. When we create, we take our emotions—our pain, our joy, our confusion—and give them a form. We turn the abstract into the tangible, the chaotic into the coherent. This process helps us understand ourselves, process our experiences, and find meaning in our struggles.

Science supports this. Studies show that creative activities like art, music, and writing can reduce stress, improve mood, and even alleviate symptoms of trauma. But beyond the science, creativity heals because it connects us to our essence. It reminds us that we're more than our pain, more than our struggles—we're creators, capable of making beauty out of brokenness.

4. Religious Teachings on Creation

Many spiritual traditions see creativity as a divine act, a reflection of the Creator's energy within us. When we create, we tap into that sacred spark.

Guru Granth Sahib Ji:

"Kudratkavankahaanvichaar."

(How can I describe the wonder of Your creation?)

This verse reminds us that creation is a divine gift. When we create, we honor the Creator within us.

Bible:

"In the beginning, God created the heavens and the earth."

— Genesis 1:1

The Bible begins with an act of creation, showing us that creativity is at the heart of existence. When we create, we align with that divine energy.

5. Creativity Beyond the Arts

Creativity isn't just about art—it's about how we live. It's in the way you arrange flowers in a vase, the way you solve a problem at work, the way you tell a story to your child. We're all creative, even if we don't think of ourselves that way. The key is to give yourself permission to play, to experiment, to make a mess.

I've seen this in my own life. I used to think I wasn't "creative" because I wasn't good at drawing or painting. But I realized that creativity shows up in other ways—like the way I write, the way I cook, the way I decorate my home. Creativity isn't about being good at something—it's about expressing yourself, however that looks.

6. A Creativity Practice

Here's a practice to help you tap into the healing power of creativity:

• Step 1: Choose a creative outlet that feels good to you. It could be writing, drawing, dancing, cooking—anything that lets you express yourself.

• Step 2: Set aside 15 minutes to create. Don't worry about the outcome—just focus on the process. For example, if you're writing, let the words flow without editing. If you're drawing, don't judge your lines.

• Step 3: Reflect on how it felt to create. Did it help you release something? Did it bring you joy? Did it connect you to yourself?

• Step 4: Keep creating. Make it a regular part of your life, even if it's just a few minutes a week.

I did this practice with gardening recently. I planted a small herb garden on my balcony, and the act of digging in the soil, watering the plants, watching them grow—it was so grounding. Creativity doesn't have to be big to be healing.

7. Creativity as a Path to Joy

Creativity isn't just about healing pain—it's about creating joy. When we create, we tap into a childlike sense of play, a lightness that reminds us life isn't all struggle. I've seen this with Meera. Her dancing didn't just help her grieve—it brought her joy. She'd laugh as she danced, her face lighting up with a happiness she hadn't felt in months.

I've experienced this too. Writing this book has been hard at times, but it's also been joyful. There's a thrill in creating something from nothing, in seeing my thoughts take shape on the page. Creativity has been my medicine, my joy, my connection to myself.

8. Sharing Your Creativity

When you create, don't be afraid to share it with the world. Your creativity isn't just for you—it's a gift to others. A poem you write might comfort someone, a meal you cook might bring people together, a dance you perform might inspire someone. Creativity connects us, heals us, reminds us of our shared humanity.

I think back to Meera's story. She started teaching dance classes at the community center, sharing her love of movement with others. Her students told her how much her classes helped them—some found joy, some found healing, some found confidence. Meera's creativity became a ripple effect of healing.

Final Words of This Chapter

Creativity is the language of your soul—speak it, and you'll find healing. It doesn't matter if you're "good" at it—what matters is that you let yourself create. Your soul has something to say, and the world needs to hear it. Pick up a pen, a paintbrush, a spatula— whatever calls to you—and create today.

Chapter 43: The Strength of Resilience

"Resilience isn't about never falling—it's about rising every time you do."

— Jagat Sandhu

1. The Inevitability of Falling

Life is full of falls—moments when we stumble, when we fail, when we feel like we can't go on. A job loss, a heartbreak, a health scare, a dream that doesn't come true—these are the moments that test us. But resilience isn't about avoiding these falls; it's about rising every time we do. It's about finding the strength to keep going, even when the road feels impossible.

I've had my share of falls. A few years ago, I applied for a writing grant that I thought would change my life. I poured my heart into the application, imagining all the ways it would help me finish this book. When I got the rejection letter, I was devastated. I felt like a failure, like I'd never be good enough. For weeks, I couldn't write—I was too consumed by self-doubt. But slowly, I started to rise. I reminded myself that rejection wasn't the end—it was a detour. I kept writing, and here we are. That fall taught me resilience.

2. A Story of Rising

Let me tell you about my cousin Simran, who embodies resilience. Simran had always dreamed of opening her own restaurant. She saved for years, found the perfect location, and poured her heart into every detail—the menu, the decor, the staff. But just three months after opening, a fire broke out in the kitchen. The restaurant was destroyed, and Simran lost everything. She was heartbroken, but she didn't give up.

Simran started over. She worked odd jobs to save money, found a new location, and rebuilt her restaurant from scratch. It took two years, but she did it. When she reopened, her community showed up in droves to support her. Simran told me, "That fire broke my heart, but it didn't break my spirit. I learned I'm stronger than I thought." Simran's story taught me that resilience isn't about never falling—it's about refusing to stay down.

3. Why Resilience Matters

Resilience matters because life will always throw challenges our way. We can't control what happens to us, but we can control how we respond. Resilience is the bridge between struggle and growth, between pain and purpose. It's what allows us to turn our wounds into wisdom, our setbacks into comebacks.

I've seen this in my own life. That rejection from the writing grant hurt, but it also taught me perseverance. It taught me to keep going, even when I didn't feel like it. It taught me that my worth isn't tied to external validation—it's tied to my own commitment to my dreams. Resilience didn't just help me recover; it helped me grow.

4. Religious Teachings on Perseverance

Spiritual traditions remind us that resilience is a sacred quality, one that helps us navigate life's inevitable challenges with grace and faith.

Quran:

"So verily, with the hardship, there is relief."

— SurahAsh-Sharh 94:6

This verse teaches that challenges are temporary, and resilience will lead us to ease. Keep going—the light is coming.

Bhagavad Gita:

"The soul is neither born, nor does it die; it is eternal."

— Chapter 2, Verse 20

The Gita reminds us that our essence is unbreakable. No matter how many times we fall, our spirit remains whole.

5. Building Resilience Through Self-Compassion

Resilience isn't about being tough all the time—it's about being kind to yourself when you fall. Self-compassion is the foundation of resilience. When you're gentle with yourself, you give yourself the strength to rise again.

I learned this after my grant rejection. At first, I was harsh with myself, thinking, "You're not good enough. You'll never make it." But those thoughts only kept me down. When I started practicing self-compassion—telling myself, "It's okay to fail. You're still worthy. Keep going"—I found the strength to rise. Self-compassion didn't make me weak; it made me resilient.

6. A Resilience Practice

Here's a practice to help you build resilience:

• Step 1: Think of a recent challenge or "fall" you've experienced. Write down what happened and how it made you feel.

• Step 2: Write a compassionate letter to yourself about that challenge. For example, "Dear Jagat, I know that rejection hurt, but it doesn't define you. You're still a writer, still worthy, still on your path."

- Step 3: Identify one small step you can take to rise again. Maybe it's trying again, seeking support, or simply resting.

- Step 4: Take that step, and celebrate yourself for rising. Reflect on how it feels to keep going.

I did this practice after a recent setback—a chapter I wrote that just wasn't working. I felt frustrated, but I wrote myself a compassionate letter, reminding myself that writing is a process. I took a small step—rewriting one paragraph—and it gave me the momentum to keep going.

7. Resilience as a Collective Strength

Resilience isn't just individual—it's collective. When we rise, we inspire others to rise too. Simran's restaurant reopening wasn't just her victory—it was her community's victory. They rallied around her, inspired by her resilience, and together, they celebrated her comeback.

I've seen this in my own life. When I shared my struggles with writing this book, my friends told me how much my perseverance inspired them. One friend said, "Seeing you keep going, even when it's hard, makes me believe I can too." Resilience is contagious—it lifts us all.

8. Rising, Again and Again

Resilience isn't a one-time act—it's a lifelong practice. You'll fall again, and that's okay. What matters is that you rise, again and again. Each time you do, you grow stronger, wiser, more capable. Each fall is a lesson, each rise a victory.

I think back to Simran's story. She didn't just rise once—she rose every day, through every challenge, through every doubt. Her resilience didn't just rebuild her restaurant; it rebuilt her spirit. It can rebuild yours too.

Final Words of This Chapter

Resilience isn't about never falling—it's about rising every time you do. You're stronger than you think, braver than you feel, more capable than you know. The next time you fall, don't stay down. Rise, dust yourself off, and keep going. The world needs your comeback—what will you rise for today?

Chapter 44: The Power of Presence

"The present moment is the only place where life truly happens—
be here, now."

— Jagat Sandhu

1. The Trap of Past and Future

We spend so much of our lives caught between the past and the
future. We dwell on what's already happened—regretting
mistakes, replaying conversations, holding onto pain. Or we worry
about what's to come—planning, stressing, imagining worst-case
scenarios. But in doing so, we miss the only moment that's real:
the present. The present moment is where life truly happens,
where we can find peace, joy, and connection.

I've fallen into this trap countless times. I'd lie awake at night,
replaying a mistake I made at work, or worrying about a deadline
that was weeks away. My mind was everywhere but here. It wasn't
until I started practicing presence that I realized how much I was
missing—the warmth of the sun on my skin, the sound of my
sister's laughter, the taste of my morning tea. Presence brought me
back to life.

2. A Story of Being Here

Let me tell you about my friend Anil, who taught me the power of
presence. Anil was always a worrier. He'd stress about his job, his
finances, his future, to the point where he couldn't enjoy the
moment. One day, he was playing with his daughter at the park,
but his mind was elsewhere—thinking about a work project due
the next week. His daughter tugged at his sleeve and said, "Daddy,
you're not here." Those words hit him hard.

Anil decided to change. He started practicing mindfulness, focusing on being fully present in each moment. The next time he took his daughter to the park, he left his phone in the car and gave her his full attention. They laughed, ran, played on the swings. Anil told me, "I felt so alive in that moment. I realized I'd been missing so much by not being present." Presence didn't just change Anil's day—it changed his relationship with his daughter, with himself, with life.

3. Why Presence Matters

Presence matters because it's the only place where we can truly live. The past is gone, the future isn't here yet—all we have is now. When we're present, we experience life fully—we notice the beauty, feel the emotions, connect with the people around us. Presence also reduces stress. When we stop dwelling on the past or worrying about the future, we give our minds a break. We find peace in the here and now.

I've seen this in my own life. When I'm present, I'm calmer, more focused, more grateful. I'll sit with a friend and really listen, instead of thinking about what I need to do next. I'll eat a meal and savor every bite, instead of rushing through it. Presence doesn't change my circumstances, but it changes how I experience them.

4. Religious Teachings on the Present

Spiritual traditions emphasize the importance of living in the present moment. They remind us that God, peace, and truth are found in the now.

Bhagavad Gita:

"Whatever you do, offer it to Me, and be free from attachment."

— Chapter 9, Verse 27

The Gita teaches us to focus on the present action, not the outcome. When we're fully present in what we're doing, we align with the divine.

Bible:

"Therefore do not worry about tomorrow, for tomorrow will worry about itself."

— Matthew 6:34

This verse reminds us to trust in the present moment. God is with us now—let's meet Him here.

5. The Barriers to Presence

Presence is simple, but it's not always easy. Our minds are wired to wander—to dwell on the past, to plan for the future. We're also surrounded by distractions—phones, notifications, endless to-do lists. It takes intention to be present, to choose the moment over the noise.

I've struggled with this myself. My phone is a constant distraction—I'll catch myself scrolling through social media when I'm supposed to be spending time with family. But I've learned that presence is a practice. It's about catching yourself when you wander and gently bringing yourself back to the moment.

6. A Presence Practice

Here's a practice to help you cultivate presence:

• Step 1: Pause wherever you are, right now. Take a deep breath and notice your surroundings.

• Step 2: Engage your senses. What do you see? Hear? Smell? Feel? Taste? For example, I might notice the sound of birds outside, the warmth of my coffee mug, the softness of my chair.

• Step 3: Let go of thoughts about the past or future. If they come up, acknowledge them, then return to the present. Say to yourself, "I am here, now."

• Step 4: Spend 1–2 minutes in this state of presence. Reflect on how it feels to be fully here.

I do this practice several times a day, especially when I feel stressed. It's a small act, but it brings me back to myself, back to the moment, back to life.

7. Presence in Relationships

Presence is especially powerful in relationships. When you're fully present with someone, you make them feel seen, heard, loved. I've noticed this with my parents. I used to visit them but be distracted—checking my phone, thinking about work. Now, I make a point to put my phone away and really be with them. I listen to their stories, ask questions, share laughter. Those moments mean so much more to all of us.

Anil's story is a perfect example. When he started being present with his daughter, their relationship deepened. She felt his love in a way she hadn't before, and he felt hers. Presence isn't just a gift to yourself—it's a gift to the people you love.

8. Living a Present Life

Presence isn't just about moments—it's about a way of life. It's about choosing to show up fully for your days, your relationships, your experiences. It's about savoring the small joys, facing the hard moments, and knowing that this moment, right now, is enough.

I think back to Anil's story. His daughter's words—"Daddy, you're not here"—became his mantra for change. He didn't just become more present at the park; he became more present in every part of his life. Presence gave him a richer, fuller, more meaningful life. It can do the same for you.

Final Words of This Chapter

The present moment is the only place where life truly happens—be here, now. Don't let the past steal your peace or the future steal your joy. Show up for this moment, with all your senses, all your heart. What can you notice, right now, that reminds you you're alive?

Chapter 45: The Gift of Self-Love

"You cannot pour from an empty cup—love yourself first, and you'll have more to give."

— Jagat Sandhu

1. The Foundation of Self-Love

Self-love is the foundation of a fulfilling life. It's the belief that you are worthy, just as you are—not because of what you do, but because of who you are. It's the practice of treating yourself with the same kindness, compassion, and care you'd offer a dear friend. But for many of us, self-love doesn't come easily. We're quick to criticize ourselves, to focus on our flaws, to feel like we're not enough.

I've struggled with self-love for most of my life. I used to think I had to earn my worth—through achievements, through pleasing others, through being "perfect." When I made a mistake, I'd berate myself for days. When I looked in the mirror, I'd see only my flaws. It wasn't until I started practicing self-love that I realized how much I'd been hurting myself—and how much I deserved my own kindness.

2. A Story of Self-Acceptance

Let me tell you about my friend Kavita, who learned to love herself after years of struggle. Kavita grew up in a family that valued appearance above all else. Her mother would comment on her weight, her skin, her clothes, always pushing her to be "prettier." Kavita internalized those messages—she felt like she was never good enough, never beautiful enough. She'd spend hours trying to "fix" herself, but nothing worked. She hated what she saw in the mirror.

After her divorce, Kavita hit rock bottom. She felt like a failure in every way. But she decided to seek help. Through therapy, she started practicing self-love. She'd look in the mirror and say, "I love you, just as you are." At first, it felt awkward, even fake. But over time, she started to believe it. She started treating herself with kindness—eating foods that nourished her, resting when she was tired, surrounding herself with people who lifted her up. Kavita told me, "Loving myself didn't change how I look—it changed how I see." Self-love gave Kavita a new lens, one of compassion and acceptance.

3. Why Self-Love Matters

Self-love matters because it's the root of everything else—your relationships, your happiness, your resilience. When you love yourself, you set healthy boundaries, you pursue your dreams, you show up authentically. You also have more to give others. You cannot pour from an empty cup—if you're depleted, you can't be there for the people you love.

I've seen this in my own life. When I started practicing self-love, my relationships improved. I stopped seeking validation from others because I was giving it to myself. I became a better friend, a better sister, a better daughter—not because I was trying harder, but because I was filled with my own love.

4. Religious Teachings on Self-Worth

Spiritual traditions remind us that we are inherently worthy, created in the image of the divine. Self-love isn't selfish—it's a sacred act.

Guru Granth Sahib Ji:

"Sabhkichh tera, tera hai, Nanak."

(Everything is Yours, everything belongs to You, O Nanak.)

This teaching reminds us that we are God's creation, worthy of love and care. Loving ourselves is a way of honoring the divine within us.

Bible:

"Love your neighbor as yourself."

— Mark 12:31

This verse often focuses on loving others, but it also implies loving yourself. You can't love your neighbor fully if you don't first love yourself.

5. The Barriers to Self-Love

Self-love is hard because we're conditioned to be hard on ourselves. Society tells us we're not enough—not thin enough, not successful enough, not perfect enough. We internalize those messages, and they become the voice in our heads. We also confuse self-love with selfishness, thinking that caring for ourselves takes away from others. But the opposite is true—self-love gives us more to share.

I've struggled with these barriers. I used to think self-love meant I was being vain or self-centered. But I realized that self-love isn't about thinking you're better than others—it's about knowing you're equal to them, deserving of the same love and care.

6. A Self-Love Practice

Here's a practice to help you cultivate self-love:

- Step 1: Stand in front of a mirror and look into your own eyes. Take a deep breath.

- Step 2: Say to yourself, "I love you, just as you are. You are enough." If it feels hard, that's okay—keep going.

- Step 3: Write down three things you love about yourself. They could be qualities (like your kindness), achievements (like your perseverance), or even small things (like your smile).

- Step 4: Throughout the day, treat yourself with kindness. Rest when you're tired, eat something nourishing, speak to yourself gently. Reflect on how it feels to be your own best friend.

I do this practice every morning, and it's transformed how I see myself. I used to focus on my flaws, but now I focus on my strengths. I'm not perfect, but I'm learning to love myself anyway.

7. Self-Love in Action

Self-love isn't just a feeling—it's an action. It's the way you talk to yourself, the boundaries you set, the choices you make. It's saying no to things that drain you, yes to things that light you up. It's forgiving yourself for your mistakes, celebrating yourself for your wins. It's showing up for yourself, day after day.

Kavita's story is a perfect example. Self-love for her meant setting boundaries with her family, surrounding herself with people who valued her for who she was, not how she looked. It meant choosing herself, even when it was hard. Self-love didn't just change her mindset—it changed her life.

8. The Ripple Effect of Self-Love

When you love yourself, you give others permission to do the same. You become a mirror, reflecting worthiness, compassion, and authenticity. I've seen this with Kavita. As she started loving herself, her friends noticed. They saw her confidence, her peace, her joy, and they wanted that for themselves. One friend told her, "You've inspired me to be kinder to myself." Self-love isn't just for you—it's for the world.

Final Words of This Chapter

You cannot pour from an empty cup—love yourself first, and you'll have more to give. You are worthy, just as you are, and you deserve your own kindness. Treat yourself like someone you love, because you are. What's one way you can show yourself love today?

Chapter 46: The Power of Letting Go

"Letting go doesn't mean giving up—it means making space for what's meant to be."

— Jagat Sandhu

1. The Burden of Holding On

We hold onto so much in life—grudges, regrets, fears, old dreams that no longer fit. We hold on because we think it keeps us safe, because we're afraid of what letting go might mean. But holding on is like carrying a heavy backpack everywhere you go—it weighs you down, slows you down, keeps you stuck. Letting go doesn't mean giving up; it means making space for what's meant to be.

I've held onto things that no longer served me. After my breakup, I held onto the hope that my ex would come back, that we'd fix things. I'd replay our memories, cling to what could have been, even though I knew deep down it was over. That holding on kept me stuck—I couldn't move forward, couldn't open myself to new love. It wasn't until I let go that I found peace, and eventually, a new relationship that was healthier and happier.

2. A Story of Release

Let me tell you about my friend Neeraj, who learned the power of letting go. Neeraj had a falling out with his brother over a family business. They stopped speaking, and Neeraj held onto his anger for years. He'd think about the argument, feel the resentment, and let it poison his peace. It affected his health, his relationships, his happiness.

One day, Neeraj decided he couldn't carry the burden anymore. He wrote his brother a letter—not to send, but to release. He poured out his anger, his hurt, his longing for reconciliation. Then he burned the letter, visualizing the resentment leaving his body. Neeraj told me, "I felt so light after that. I realized I wasn't letting go for him—I was letting go for me." A few months later, his brother reached out, and they started rebuilding their relationship. Letting go didn't just free Neeraj—it opened the door for healing.

3. Why Letting Go Feels Hard

Letting go feels hard because it requires us to surrender control. We hold onto things because we think they define us, because we're afraid of the unknown, because we don't trust that something better might come. But holding on often keeps us tied to pain, to the past, to a version of ourselves that no longer exists.

I've felt this resistance myself. Letting go of my ex was hard because I was afraid of being alone, afraid I'd never find love again. But I realized that holding on was keeping me in a cycle of pain. Letting go was scary, but it was also liberating. It gave me the space to heal, to grow, to love again.

4. Religious Teachings on Surrender

Spiritual traditions teach that letting go is a sacred act of surrender, a way to trust in a higher plan.

Bhagavad Gita:

"Abandon all varieties of religion and just surrender unto Me. I shall deliver you from all sinful reactions."

— Chapter 18, Verse 66

The Gita teaches that letting go of our attachments and surrendering to God brings liberation.

Quran:

"And whoever relies upon Allah—then He is sufficient for him."

— SurahAt-Talaq 65:3

This verse reminds us to let go of our need to control and trust in Allah's plan. When we surrender, we find peace.

5. What We Gain When We Let Go

When we let go, we gain so much—peace, freedom, space for new possibilities. Letting go of my ex allowed me to rediscover myself. I started writing again, reconnecting with friends, exploring new hobbies. I found joy in my own company, and eventually, I found a new love that was better than I could have imagined. Letting go didn't take away from me—it added to me.

I've seen this with Neeraj too. Letting go of his anger didn't just free him from resentment—it freed him to rebuild his relationship with his brother. It gave him back his peace, his health, his happiness. Letting go isn't losing—it's gaining.

6. A Letting Go Practice

Here's a practice to help you let go of something that's weighing you down:

• Step 1: Identify something you're holding onto—a grudge, a regret, a fear. Write it down in detail.

- Step 2: Visualize it as a heavy object in your hands. Feel its weight, its burden.

- Step 3: Imagine setting it down, letting it go into the earth, the universe, or God's hands. Say to yourself, "I release this. I make space for what's meant to be."

- Step 4: Take a deep breath and notice how you feel. Reflect on the lightness, the freedom, the space you've created.

I did this practice with a fear I was holding onto—the fear of failure with this book. Visualizing it as a heavy stone and letting it go helped me feel lighter, more confident. Letting go gave me the courage to keep writing.

7. Letting Go as a Daily Practice

Letting go isn't a one-time act—it's a daily practice. Every day, we have the chance to release what no longer serves us—small frustrations, old stories, limiting beliefs. It's about choosing freedom over and over again.

I've made letting go a part of my routine. At the end of each day, I reflect on what I need to release—maybe it's a harsh word I said to myself, maybe it's a worry about tomorrow. I write it down, visualize letting it go, and go to bed lighter. It's a small act, but it's powerful.

8. The Space for What's Meant to Be

When we let go, we make space for what's meant to be—new opportunities, new relationships, new versions of ourselves. Neeraj's story is a perfect example. Letting go of his anger didn't just free him—it opened the door for reconciliation with his brother. It made space for love, for healing, for a better future.

I think back to my own journey. Letting go of my ex made space for a new love, a new chapter, a new me. Letting go isn't the end—it's the beginning.

Final Words of This Chapter

Letting go doesn't mean giving up—it means making space for what's meant to be. Release the burdens you've been carrying, and trust that something better is waiting. You deserve peace, freedom, and a life that feels light. What can you let go of today?

Chapter 47: The Strength of Hope

"Hope is the light that guides you through the darkest nights—hold onto it, always."

— Jagat Sandhu

1. The Lifeline of Hope

Hope is the belief that things can get better, that there's light at the end of the tunnel, that tomorrow holds possibilities. It's the lifeline that keeps us going through the darkest nights—the loss of a loved one, the failure of a dream, the weight of despair. Hope doesn't erase our pain, but it gives us the strength to carry it, the courage to keep moving forward.

I've clung to hope during some of my hardest moments. When I lost my friend to illness, I felt like I'd never smile again. The grief was suffocating, and I couldn't imagine a future without him. But hope whispered to me, "You'll heal. You'll find joy again." It wasn't loud, it wasn't certain, but it was enough to get me out of bed each day. Slowly, hope became reality—I did heal, I did find joy. Hope didn't just comfort me; it carried me.

2. A Story of Holding On

Let me tell you about my neighbor, Mrs. Sharma, who showed me the strength of hope. Mrs. Sharma's husband was diagnosed with cancer, and the prognosis wasn't good. She was devastated, but she refused to give up hope. She'd sit by his bedside, holding his hand, telling him stories of the future—trips they'd take, meals they'd cook, memories they'd make. She'd pray every day, not just for a miracle, but for the strength to face whatever came.

Miraculously, her husband's treatment worked. He went into remission, and they celebrated every small victory—a walk in the park, a shared meal, a quiet evening together. Mrs. Sharma told me, "Hope kept me going when I wanted to give up. It gave me a reason to fight." Her story taught me that hope isn't passive—it's a powerful force, one that fuels action, resilience, and love.

3. Why Hope Matters

Hope matters because it's the antidote to despair. It's what keeps us going when everything feels lost. Studies show that hope has tangible benefits—it reduces stress, improves mental health, and even boosts physical healing. But beyond the science, hope matters because it's the spark of possibility. It's the belief that no matter how dark the night, the dawn will come.

I've seen this in my own life. During a financial struggle, I felt hopeless—I didn't know how I'd pay my bills, how I'd keep going. But hope reminded me that I'd faced challenges before and come through. It pushed me to take action—to look for new opportunities, to ask for help, to keep believing in myself. Hope didn't solve my problems, but it gave me the strength to solve them.

4. Religious Teachings on Hope

Spiritual traditions teach that hope is a sacred gift, a reflection of faith in a higher power.

Quran:

"Do not despair of the mercy of Allah."

— SurahAz-Zumar 39:53

This verse reminds us that no matter how hard things get, God's mercy is always there. Hope is a way of trusting in that mercy.

Bible:

"May the God of hope fill you with all joy and peace as you trust in Him."

— Romans 15:13

This verse teaches that hope comes from faith. When we trust in God, we find the hope to keep going.

5. Hope in the Face of Uncertainty

Hope doesn't mean ignoring reality—it means believing in possibility, even in the face of uncertainty. Mrs. Sharma didn't know if her husband would survive, but she hoped anyway. She hoped for healing, but she also hoped for strength, for love, for meaning. Hope isn't about guarantees; it's about faith.

I've learned this through my own experiences. When I started writing this book, I didn't know if it would succeed. There were no guarantees—no publisher, no audience, no certainty. But I hoped. I hoped that my words would resonate, that they'd help someone, that they'd fulfill my purpose. That hope kept me writing, even when I doubted myself.

6. A Hope Practice

Here's a practice to help you cultivate hope:

• Step 1: Think of a challenge you're facing right now. Write down how it's making you feel.

• Step 2: Imagine a hopeful outcome. What would it look like if things got better? Be specific—picture the details, feel the emotions.

• Step 3: Write down one small action you can take to move toward that outcome. It could be asking for help, taking a small step, or simply praying.

• Step 4: Take that action, and hold onto the hope that things can improve. Reflect on how hope feels in your body, your heart.

I did this practice during a recent health scare. I was worried about a test result, and I felt overwhelmed. I imagined a hopeful outcome—good news, a clean bill of health—and I took a small action: I called a friend for support. That hope, that action, helped me through the waiting. (The results were fine, by the way.)

7. Hope as a Collective Force

Hope isn't just individual—it's collective. When we hold onto hope, we inspire others to do the same. Mrs. Sharma's hope didn't just sustain her—it sustained her husband, her family, her community. They saw her faith, her love, her strength, and it gave them hope too.

I've seen this in my own life. When I shared my hope for this book with my friends, they started hoping with me. They'd say, "I can't wait to read it," or "I know it's going to help so many people." Their hope fueled mine, and together, we kept going. Hope is a light that spreads.

8. Holding Onto Hope, Always

Hope is a choice, one you can make every day. Some days, it'll feel easy; other days, it'll feel hard. But no matter what, hold onto it.

It's the light that guides you through the darkest nights, the whisper that says, "Keep going."

I think back to Mrs. Sharma's story. Her hope wasn't just about her husband's survival—it was about their love, their resilience, their shared journey. Hope gave her the strength to face every day, and it gave her a miracle. It can give you one too.

Final Words of This Chapter

Hope is the light that guides you through the darkest nights—hold onto it, always. It's the spark that keeps you going, the faith that things can get better, the belief that you're stronger than you know. What are you hoping for today? Let that hope carry you forward.

Chapter 48: The Power of Authenticity

"Be yourself—everyone else is already taken."

— Jagat Sandhu

1. The Masks We Wear

We live in a world that often asks us to be someone we're not. We wear masks to fit in, to be liked, to avoid judgment. We hide our true selves—our quirks, our passions, our vulnerabilities—because we're afraid of being rejected. But living behind a mask is exhausting. It keeps us from the joy, connection, and freedom that come with authenticity.

I've worn my share of masks. In my early twenties, I tried to be the "perfect" daughter, friend, employee. I'd say what I thought people wanted to hear, do what I thought they wanted me to do, even if it meant ignoring my own truth. I thought that's what it meant to be loved. But the more I hid, the more disconnected I felt—from others, from myself. It wasn't until I started being authentic that I found real belonging.

2. A Story of True Self

Let me tell you about my friend Sonia, who embraced her authenticity and found freedom. Sonia was always the "funny one" in her friend group. She'd make people laugh, always putting on a happy face, even when she was struggling. Deep down, she was an introvert who loved quiet nights with a book, but she felt like she had to be the life of the party to be loved.

One day, Sonia decided she couldn't keep up the act. She started showing her true self—she'd say no to parties she didn't want to attend, share her love of literature, admit when she was feeling down. At first, she worried her friends would drift away, but the opposite happened. They loved her even more. They said, "We feel like we're really seeing you now." Sonia told me, "Being myself was scary, but it was also the most freeing thing I've ever done." Authenticity didn't push people away—it brought them closer.

3. Why Authenticity Matters

Authenticity matters because it's the key to a meaningful life. When you're authentic, you live in alignment with your values, your passions, your truth. You attract people who love you for you, not for who you pretend to be. You also give others permission to be authentic—your courage inspires theirs.

I've seen this in my own life. When I started being authentic—sharing my struggles, my dreams, my quirks—I noticed a shift in my relationships. My friends opened up more, our conversations got deeper, our connection grew stronger. Authenticity didn't just make me feel free; it made my relationships richer.

4. Religious Teachings on Truth

Spiritual traditions emphasize the importance of living truthfully, of being who you were created to be.

Guru Granth Sahib Ji:

"Sachbol, sach sun, sachkar."

(Speak the truth, hear the truth, live the truth.)

This teaching reminds us that authenticity is a sacred act. When we live our truth, we honor the divine within us.

Bible:

"The truth will set you free."

— John 8:32

This verse teaches that living authentically—being true to yourself—brings freedom and peace.

5. The Cost of Inauthenticity

Living inauthentically comes at a cost. It costs you your peace, your joy, your sense of self. When you're constantly pretending, you lose touch with who you are. You become a shadow of yourself, living for others instead of for you.

I've felt this cost. When I was wearing my "perfect" mask, I was miserable. I felt like a fraud, always worried that someone would see through me. I'd go to bed exhausted, not from what I'd done, but from who I'd been pretending to be. Authenticity gave me back my energy, my joy, my life.

6. An Authenticity Practice

Here's a practice to help you embrace your authentic self:

• Step 1: Reflect on a time when you felt truly yourself—when you weren't trying to be anyone else. What were you doing? Who were you with? How did it feel?

• Step 2: Write down three things that make you, you. Maybe it's your sense of humor, your love of nature, your quiet strength.

• Step 3: Share one of those things with someone today. For example, if you love poetry, share a poem with a friend. If you're a dreamer, tell someone about a dream you have.

- Step 4: Reflect on how it felt to be authentic. Did it feel freeing? Did it deepen your connection?

I did this practice recently. I shared my love of writing with a new friend, telling her about this book. I was nervous, but she was so supportive. Being authentic didn't just feel good—it built a new connection.

7. Authenticity in a Judgmental World

Being authentic isn't always easy. The world can be judgmental, and not everyone will accept your true self. But the right people will—the ones who matter, the ones who see you and love you for you. And even if some people don't accept you, authenticity is still worth it. It's better to be rejected for who you are than loved for who you're not.

Sonia's story is a testament to this. When she started being her introverted, book-loving self, a few friends drifted away. But the ones who stayed became her true tribe. Authenticity didn't just give her freedom—it gave her the right relationships.

8. The Freedom of Being You

Authenticity is the ultimate freedom. It's the freedom to show up as you are, to live your truth, to love yourself fully. When you're authentic, you don't have to hide, pretend, or shrink. You get to be you—gloriously, unapologetically you.

I think back to Sonia's story. Being authentic didn't just change her relationships—it changed her. She became more confident, more joyful, more at peace. Authenticity gave her the freedom to live a life that was truly hers. It can do the same for you.

Final Words of This Chapter

Be yourself—everyone else is already taken. The world doesn't need another copy—it needs you, in all your unique, authentic glory. Take off the mask, show up as you are, and watch how it sets you free. What's one way you can be more authentic today?

Chapter 49: The Power of Joy

"Joy is not the absence of pain—it's the courage to find light in the midst of it."

— Jagat Sandhu

4. Joy as a Lifeline (Continued)

was a lifeline. It reminded me that even in my struggles, there was still beauty to be found, still reasons to smile.

5. Religious Teachings on Joy

Spiritual traditions remind us that joy is a sacred state, one that connects us to the divine and to our true nature.

Guru Granth Sahib Ji:

"Anand bhaiamerimaae, Satguru mai paia."

(I am in bliss, O my mother, for I have found my True Guru.)

This verse teaches that true joy comes from connecting with the divine, from aligning with our higher purpose.

Bible:

"The joy of the Lord is your strength."

— Nehemiah 8:10

This verse reminds us that joy isn't just a feeling—it's a source of strength. When we tap into divine joy, we find the resilience to face any challenge.

6. Finding Joy in the Everyday

Joy doesn't have to be big or dramatic. It's often in the small, quiet moments—the smell of rain, the sound of a loved one's voice, the warmth of a cozy blanket. We just have to train ourselves to notice it, to savor it, to let it fill us up.

I've made it a habit to seek out these moments. Every evening, I take a few minutes to reflect on something that brought me joy that day. Sometimes it's a conversation with a friend, sometimes it's the way the sky looked at sunset, sometimes it's just the fact that I made it through a tough day. This practice has changed the way I experience life—it's taught me that joy is always there, waiting to be found.

7. A Joy Practice

Here's a practice to help you cultivate joy in your life:

• Step 1: At the end of each day, write down three things that brought you joy. They can be big or small—a kind word, a good meal, a moment of laughter.

• Step 2: Reflect on why those moments brought you joy. What did they make you feel? What did they remind you of?

• Step 3: Share one of those moments with someone—a friend, a family member, or even on social media. Spreading joy multiplies it.

• Step 4: Make a commitment to notice joy tomorrow. Look for it in the small things, and let it light up your day.

I started doing this practice after Ravi shared his story with me. One day, I wrote down: "The sound of my nephew giggling, the taste of my mom's homemade paratha, the feeling of the breeze on my walk." Reflecting on those moments made me feel so grateful, so alive. Joy isn't hard to find—it's just a matter of looking.

8. Joy as a Rebellion

Choosing joy is an act of rebellion in a world that often focuses on what's wrong. It's a way of saying, "I refuse to let my circumstances define me. I will find light, even in the dark." Ravi's story is a perfect example of this. Despite his illness, despite his pain, he chose joy. He rebelled against despair, and in doing so, he found a way to live fully, even in his struggle.

I've tried to adopt this rebellious spirit in my own life. When I'm having a hard day—maybe I'm stressed about a deadline or feeling overwhelmed—I'll pause and find a reason to smile. I'll put on a song that makes me dance, or I'll call a friend who always makes me laugh. Joy isn't just a feeling for me anymore—it's a choice, a stand, a way of reclaiming my power.

Final Words of This Chapter

Joy is not the absence of pain—it's the courage to find light in the midst of it. You don't have to wait for the perfect moment to feel joy—you can choose it right now, in the mess, in the struggle, in the ordinary. Look for the light today, and let it guide you. What brought you joy today?

Chapter 50: The Strength of Boundaries

"Boundaries are the walls that protect your peace—build them with love, not fear."

— Jagat Sandhu

1. The Importance of Boundaries

Boundaries are the invisible walls we build to protect our peace, our energy, our well-being. They're the lines we draw to say, "This is what I'm okay with, and this is what I'm not." But for many of us, setting boundaries feels hard. We worry about disappointing others, seeming selfish, or creating conflict. Yet boundaries aren't about pushing people away—they're about creating space for healthy relationships, for self-respect, for a life that feels good.

I used to struggle with boundaries. I'd say yes to everything—every invitation, every request, every demand—because I didn't want to let anyone down. But I was letting myself down. I'd end up exhausted, resentful, and disconnected from my own needs. It wasn't until I started setting boundaries that I realized how much I'd been giving away my power—and how much I could reclaim by saying no.

2. A Story of Self-Respect

Let me tell you about my friend Aarti, who learned the power of boundaries after years of over-giving. Aarti was the kind of person everyone relied on—her family, her friends, her colleagues. She'd drop everything to help someone, even if it meant sacrificing her own time, energy, or well-being. But over time, she started to feel drained. She'd snap at the people she loved, feel overwhelmed by her to-do list, and resent the very people she was trying to help.

Aarti decided she needed to change. She started small—she told her family she needed one evening a week to herself, no interruptions. At first, they pushed back, but she held firm. She explained, "I love you, but I need this to be my best for you." Over time, she set more boundaries—saying no to extra projects at work, limiting how often she'd take on others' problems. Aarti told me, "Setting boundaries didn't make me selfish—it made me whole. I had more to give because I wasn't giving everything away." Her story taught me that boundaries aren't about exclusion—they're about self-respect.

3. Why Boundaries Matter

Boundaries matter because they protect what's sacred—your time, your energy, your peace. Without them, you risk burnout, resentment, and a life that feels out of alignment. Boundaries also create healthier relationships. When you're clear about your needs, you give others the chance to respect them, and you build connections based on mutual care, not obligation.

I've seen this in my own life. When I started setting boundaries, my relationships improved. I used to feel guilty saying no to friends, but once I started, I noticed they respected me more. They saw that I valued myself, and that made them value me too. Boundaries didn't push people away—they brought us closer, in a more authentic way.

4. Religious Teachings on Self-Care

Spiritual traditions remind us that caring for ourselves—through boundaries—is a sacred act, one that allows us to serve others more fully.

Quran:

"Do not throw yourselves into destruction with your own hands."

— SurahAl-Baqarah 2:195

This verse teaches that self-preservation is important. Setting boundaries ensures we don't harm ourselves by overextending.

Guru Granth Sahib Ji:

"Aap japo, avrehnaamjapaao."

(Meditate on the divine yourself, and inspire others to do the same.)

This teaching reminds us to prioritize our own spiritual well-being. Boundaries allow us to nurture ourselves so we can uplift others.

5. The Fear of Setting Boundaries

Setting boundaries can feel scary because we're afraid of how others will react. We worry they'll be upset, that they'll think we're selfish, that they'll leave. But the right people will respect your boundaries—and the ones who don't might not belong in your life. Boundaries aren't about fear—they're about love, for yourself and for others.

I've felt this fear myself. The first time I told a friend I couldn't help with something, I was terrified she'd be mad. But she wasn't—she said, "I'm glad you told me. I don't want you to feel overwhelmed." That moment taught me that boundaries don't destroy relationships—they strengthen them.

6. A Boundary Practice

Here's a practice to help you set and maintain boundaries:

• Step 1: Reflect on an area of your life where you feel drained or resentful. Is there a person, situation, or habit that's crossing your boundaries?

• Step 2: Decide on a clear boundary. For example, "I won't take work calls after 7 p.m.," or "I need one hour a day to myself."

• Step 3: Communicate your boundary with love. Use "I" statements, like, "I need this to feel my best," rather than blaming the other person.

• Step 4: Stick to your boundary, even if it feels uncomfortable at first. Reflect on how it feels to protect your peace.

I did this practice with my family. I told them I needed Sunday mornings to write, uninterrupted. At first, they'd still call or ask for help, but I gently reminded them of my boundary. Now, they respect it, and I feel so much more balanced. Boundaries have given me back my peace.

7. Boundaries as an Act of Love

Boundaries aren't just for you—they're for the people you love. When you set boundaries, you show up as your best self, not a depleted version of yourself. You're able to give more fully, more joyfully, because you're not running on empty.

Aarti's story is a perfect example. When she started setting boundaries, she thought her family would feel neglected. But instead, they noticed how much happier she was, how much more present. Her boundaries didn't take away from her love—they amplified it.

8. The Freedom of Boundaries

Boundaries give you freedom—the freedom to say yes to what matters, the freedom to live a life that feels good, the freedom to be yourself. They're the walls that protect your peace, but they're also the doors that let in the right kind of love, the right kind of energy.

I think back to Aarti's story. Her boundaries didn't just protect her—they liberated her. She became more herself, more vibrant, more alive. Boundaries didn't limit her life—they expanded it. They can do the same for you.

Final Words of This Chapter

Boundaries are the walls that protect your peace—build them with love, not fear. You deserve a life that feels good, relationships that feel mutual, energy that feels abundant. Set a boundary today, and watch how it sets you free. What boundary do you need to set right now?

Chapter 51: The Power of Forgiveness

"Forgiveness is the key that unlocks the cage of your heart—set yourself free."

— Jagat Sandhu

1. The Weight of Unforgiveness

Holding onto anger, resentment, or hurt is like carrying a heavy chain around your heart. It weighs you down, keeps you stuck, and steals your peace. Forgiveness isn't about excusing what happened—it's about freeing yourself from the burden of carrying it. It's about choosing your peace over your pain, your freedom over your past.

I've carried the weight of unforgiveness myself. A few years ago, a close friend betrayed my trust. She shared something I'd told her in confidence, and it spread, leaving me humiliated. I was furious, and I held onto that anger for months. I'd replay the betrayal in my mind, imagining confrontations, feeling the sting over and over. But all that anger didn't hurt her—it hurt me. It wasn't until I chose forgiveness that I felt free.

2. A Story of Liberation

Let me tell you about my uncle, Raj, who found freedom through forgiveness. Raj had a falling out with his business partner, who cheated him out of a significant amount of money. The betrayal ended their partnership and left Raj struggling financially. For years, he harbored resentment—he'd talk about the betrayal with bitterness, his face tightening with anger.

One day, Raj decided he couldn't carry the weight anymore. He wrote a letter to his former partner—not to send, but to release. He wrote about the hurt, the anger, the betrayal, and then he wrote, "I forgive you, not because you deserve it, but because I deserve peace." He burned the letter, and with it, he let go of the resentment. Raj told me, "Forgiveness didn't change what happened, but it changed me. I felt like I could breathe again." His story taught me that forgiveness isn't for the other person—it's for you.

3. Why Forgiveness Matters

Forgiveness matters because it's the path to inner peace. When you forgive, you release the emotional poison that's been holding you back. You stop giving your power to the person who hurt you, and you reclaim it for yourself. Forgiveness also heals relationships—sometimes it leads to reconciliation, sometimes it just leads to closure, but either way, it frees you to move forward.

I've seen this in my own life. When I forgave my friend, I didn't just let go of my anger—I let go of the hold she had on me. I was able to see her with compassion, to understand that her actions came from her own struggles, not from me. Forgiveness didn't erase the hurt, but it transformed it into a lesson, a strength, a new beginning.

4. Religious Teachings on Forgiveness

Spiritual traditions emphasize forgiveness as a sacred act, one that aligns us with divine love and mercy.

Bible:

"Forgive, and you will be forgiven."

— Luke 6:37

This verse teaches that forgiveness is a cycle—what we give, we receive. When we forgive others, we open ourselves to divine forgiveness.

Quran:

"The reward of the evil is the evil thereof, but whosoever forgives and makes peace, his reward is with Allah."

— Surah Ash-Shura 42:40

This verse reminds us that forgiveness is a noble act, one that brings us closer to God's mercy and reward.

5. Forgiveness as a Process

Forgiveness isn't a one-time act—it's a process. Some hurts are deep, and they take time to release. That's okay. Forgiveness doesn't mean you have to feel okay about what happened right away; it means you're willing to work toward peace, one step at a time.

I learned this through my own journey. Forgiving my friend didn't happen overnight. At first, I could barely think about her without feeling angry. But I started small—I'd pray for her, even when I didn't feel like it. I'd remind myself that holding onto anger was only hurting me. Slowly, the anger faded, and forgiveness took its place. It was a process, but it was worth it.

6. A Forgiveness Practice

Here's a practice to help you move toward forgiveness:

• Step 1: Think of someone you need to forgive—someone who's hurt you, big or small. Write down what happened and how it made you feel.

- Step 2: Write a letter to that person (you don't have to send it). Pour out your hurt, your anger, your pain. Then write, "I forgive you, not because you deserve it, but because I deserve peace."

- Step 3: Release the letter—burn it, tear it up, or bury it. As you do, visualize the hurt leaving your body, making space for peace.

- Step 4: Reflect on how you feel. Forgiveness is a journey, so be gentle with yourself if it takes time.

I did this practice with a colleague who had undermined me at work. Writing the letter helped me process my feelings, and releasing it helped me let go. I didn't feel completely healed right away, but I felt lighter, freer, closer to peace.

7. Forgiving Yourself

Sometimes, the hardest person to forgive is yourself. We hold onto guilt, shame, and self-blame, punishing ourselves for mistakes long after they've passed. But self-forgiveness is just as important as forgiving others—it's the key to loving yourself fully.

I've had to forgive myself for things I regret—like the times I wasn't there for a friend, or the opportunities I didn't take because of fear. I used the same forgiveness practice, writing a letter to myself, saying, "I forgive you, Jagat. You were doing your best." Self-forgiveness didn't erase my mistakes, but it allowed me to learn from them and move forward.

8. The Freedom of Forgiveness

Forgiveness is the key that unlocks the cage of your heart. It sets you free from the past, from the pain, from the chains of resentment. Raj's story is a perfect example. Forgiving his business partner didn't change the betrayal, but it changed him. It gave him back his peace, his joy, his ability to trust again.

I think back to my own journey. Forgiving my friend didn't just free me from anger—it freed me to love again, to trust again, to live again. Forgiveness isn't a gift you give to someone else—it's a gift you give to yourself.

Final Words of This Chapter

Forgiveness is the key that unlocks the cage of your heart—set yourself free. You don't have to carry the weight of resentment any longer. Choose peace, choose freedom, choose forgiveness. Who do you need to forgive today—someone else, or maybe yourself?

Chapter 52: The Strength of Patience

"Patience is the soil in which miracles grow—trust the timing of your life."

— Jagat Sandhu

1. The Challenge of Waiting

We live in a world that celebrates speed—fast food, fast results, fast success. But life doesn't always move at our pace. Sometimes, we have to wait—for a dream to come true, for a wound to heal, for a prayer to be answered. Patience is the ability to wait with grace, to trust the timing of your life, to believe that what's meant for you will come when the time is right.

I've struggled with patience my whole life. When I started writing this book, I wanted it to be done quickly. I'd set unrealistic deadlines, get frustrated when I couldn't meet them, and feel like I was failing. But I learned that creativity can't be rushed—it has its own rhythm. Patience taught me to trust the process, to keep going even when I couldn't see the finish line.

2. A Story of Trusting the Timing

Let me tell you about my friend Vikram, who learned the power of patience through a long journey. Vikram always wanted to start his own tech company, but he faced setback after setback. Investors rejected his ideas, partners backed out, and he struggled to balance his dream with financial stability. He'd often say, "I feel like I'm running out of time."

Instead of giving up, Vikram decided to be patient. He kept working on his idea, refining it, learning from each rejection. He took a day job to pay the bills but spent his evenings building his dream. After five years of persistence, he finally got the funding he needed. His company launched, and it was a success. Vikram told me, "Patience didn't just get me through—it made me better. I wouldn't have been ready if it had happened sooner." His story taught me that patience isn't just about waiting—it's about growing while you wait.

3. Why Patience Matters

Patience matters because it allows us to surrender to life's timing. It teaches us resilience, trust, and faith. When we're patient, we stop fighting against what we can't control and start focusing on what we can—our effort, our attitude, our growth. Patience also deepens our appreciation for what we receive. When we've waited for something, we value it more.

I've seen this in my own life. When I finally finished the first draft of this book—after months of slow progress—I felt such a deep sense of gratitude. The wait made the achievement sweeter. Patience didn't just help me finish—it helped me savor the journey.

4. Religious Teachings on Patience

Spiritual traditions remind us that patience is a virtue, one that aligns us with divine timing and wisdom.

Quran:

"Seek help through patience and prayer."

— SurahAl-Baqarah 2:45

This verse teaches that patience is a source of strength. When we wait with faith, we find divine support.

Bhagavad Gita:

"Perform your duty equipoised, O Arjuna, abandoning all attachment to success or failure."

— Chapter 2, Verse 48

The Gita reminds us to focus on the effort, not the outcome. Patience allows us to do our part and trust the rest to the universe.

5. Patience in the Face of Frustration

Patience isn't easy—it's often tested by frustration, doubt, and uncertainty. But those moments of struggle are where patience grows. When we choose to wait with grace, even when we're frustrated, we build a deeper resilience, a deeper faith.

I've felt this frustration myself. During a long stretch of writer's block, I wanted to give up. I'd sit at my desk, staring at a blank page, feeling like I'd never finish this book. But I kept showing up, even when it felt pointless. I'd write one sentence, then another, trusting that the words would come. And they did. Patience didn't just get me through—it taught me to trust myself.

6. A Patience Practice

Here's a practice to help you cultivate patience:

• Step 1: Think of something you're waiting for—a goal, a change, a resolution. Write down how the wait makes you feel.

• Step 2: Reflect on what you can control. What small steps can you take while you wait? For example, if you're waiting for a job offer, can you keep learning new skills?

- Step 3: Practice surrender. Say to yourself, "I trust the timing of my life. I'll do my part and let the rest unfold."

- Step 4: Find joy in the waiting. Do something that brings you peace—meditate, take a walk, listen to music. Reflect on how patience feels.

I did this practice while waiting for feedback on a chapter I'd submitted to a friend. I was anxious, but I focused on what I could control—I kept writing the next chapter. I surrendered to the timing, and I found joy in the process. When the feedback finally came, I was ready to receive it.

7. Patience as a Teacher

Patience is a teacher—it shows us how to trust, how to grow, how to let go. Vikram's story is a perfect example. The years he spent waiting for his company to take off weren't wasted—they were a classroom. He learned resilience, strategy, and self-belief. Patience didn't just bring him success—it made him ready for it.

I've learned from patience too. Writing this book taught me that good things take time. It taught me to trust my process, to believe in my vision, to keep going even when I couldn't see the end. Patience didn't just help me write—it helped me grow.

8. Trusting the Bigger Plan

Patience is an act of faith—a belief that there's a bigger plan at work, even when we can't see it. Sometimes, the things we're waiting for don't come in the way we expect, but they come in the way we need. Patience allows us to trust that everything is unfolding as it should.

I think back to Vikram's story. He thought he was running out of time, but the wait was preparing him. When his company finally launched, he was more skilled, more confident, more ready than he would have been years earlier. Patience didn't just give him his dream—it gave him the strength to sustain it.

Final Words of This Chapter

Patience is the soil in which miracles grow—trust the timing of your life. The wait might feel hard, but it's shaping you, preparing you, leading you to where you're meant to be. Keep going, keep trusting, keep growing. What are you waiting for right now, and how can you find peace in the wait?

Chapter 53: The Power of Community

"A tree stands tall because of its roots—your community is the soil that holds you steady."

— Jagat Sandhu

1. The Strength of Togetherness

No one thrives alone. We're meant to be part of a community—to support and be supported, to love and be loved, to grow together. A community is the soil that holds us steady, the roots that keep us grounded, the branches that lift us up. In a world that often feels isolating, community reminds us that we belong.

I've felt the power of community in my own life. When I started writing this book, I was terrified—I doubted myself, worried I'd fail. But my community—my family, my friends, my writing group—held me up. They'd read my drafts, offer feedback, cheer me on. Their belief in me gave me the courage to keep going. Community didn't just support me—it strengthened me.

2. A Story of Collective Support

Let me tell you about my neighbor, Maya, who experienced the power of community during a crisis. Maya was a single mother who lost her job during a tough economic period. She struggled to pay rent, buy groceries, and keep her kids in school. She felt ashamed to ask for help, but her neighbors noticed her struggle. One day, they organized a community fundraiser—everyone pitched in, some with money, others with food, clothes, or school supplies.

Maya was overwhelmed with gratitude. The fundraiser helped her get back on her feet, but more than that, it reminded her that she wasn't alone. Her community became her safety net, her family, her strength. Maya told me, "I thought I had to do it all on my own, but my community showed me what togetherness really means." Her story taught me that community isn't just about being there for the good times—it's about showing up when it matters most.

3. Why Community Matters

Community matters because it gives us a sense of belonging, purpose, and support. Studies show that people with strong social ties are happier, healthier, and more resilient. But beyond the science, community matters because it reflects our shared humanity. It reminds us that we're all connected, that we're stronger together, that we don't have to face life's challenges alone.

I've seen this in my own life. During a period of grief after losing my friend, I felt so isolated. But my community—my family, my friends, even my neighbors—rallied around me. They'd bring me meals, sit with me in silence, share stories of their own losses. Their presence didn't take away my pain, but it made it bearable. Community didn't just comfort me—it carried me.

4. Religious Teachings on Togetherness

Spiritual traditions emphasize the importance of community, reminding us that we're meant to live in harmony with others.

Guru Granth Sahib Ji:

"Sangatvich sukh hai, sangatvich shanti hai."

(In the company of the holy, there is peace and happiness.)

This teaching reminds us that community—especially one rooted in shared values—brings peace and joy.

Bible:

"Bear one another's burdens, and so fulfill the law of Christ."

— Galatians 6:2

This verse teaches that community is about mutual support. When we help each other, we live out divine love.

5. Building Your Community

Sometimes, community doesn't come ready-made—you have to build it. That means reaching out, showing up, being vulnerable. It means finding people who share your values, who lift you up, who make you feel seen.

I've had to build my own community over the years. When I moved to a new city, I didn't know anyone. I joined a book club, started chatting with my neighbors, and reconnected with old friends online. It took effort, but slowly, I built a network of people who became my family. Community isn't just something you find—it's something you create.

6. A Community Practice

Here's a practice to help you strengthen or build your community:

• Step 1: Reflect on the communities in your life—your family, friends, coworkers, neighbors. Who makes you feel supported? Who do you want to connect with more deeply?

• Step 2: Reach out to someone in your community today. It could be a phone call, a coffee date, or a simple message saying, "I'm thinking of you."

- Step 3: Offer something to your community—a listening ear, a helping hand, a kind word. Community is a two-way street.

- Step 4: Reflect on how it feels to be part of a community. How does it make you feel connected, supported, or inspired?

I did this practice with my writing group. I reached out to thank them for their support and offered to read someone's draft. That small act deepened our connection, and I felt so grateful to be part of such a supportive community.

7. Community in Times of Struggle

Community shines brightest in times of struggle. When we're going through something hard, our community becomes our strength—they hold us up, remind us we're not alone, help us find our way back to the light.

Maya's story is a perfect example. Her community didn't just give her material support—they gave her emotional support, a sense of belonging, a reason to keep going. They showed her that she didn't have to face her struggles alone. Community isn't just a luxury— it's a lifeline.

8. The Ripple Effect of Community

When you're part of a strong community, the impact ripples outward. You support each other, and that support spreads— lifting up families, neighborhoods, even the world. I think back to Maya's story. Her community's act of kindness didn't just help her—it inspired others to give, to connect, to care. One act of togetherness created a wave of goodness.

I've seen this in my own life. My writing group doesn't just support each other—we inspire each other. When one of us succeeds, we all celebrate, and it pushes us to keep going. Community isn't just about receiving—it's about giving, growing, and creating something bigger than ourselves.

Final Words of This Chapter

A tree stands tall because of its roots—your community is the soil that holds you steady. You don't have to do life alone. Reach out, show up, build the connections that lift you up. Who's in your community, and how can you strengthen those ties today?

Chapter 54: The Power of Purpose

"Purpose is the compass that guides your life—find it, and you'll never feel lost."

— Jagat Sandhu

1. The Search for Meaning

We all crave purpose—a reason to get out of bed, a direction for our lives, a sense that what we do matters. Purpose is the compass that guides us through life's uncertainties, the light that keeps us going, the anchor that grounds us. But finding purpose isn't always easy—it's a journey of self-discovery, reflection, and courage.

I've searched for purpose my whole life. For years, I thought it was about my career—I chased success, thinking that a prestigious job would make me feel fulfilled. But even when I achieved my goals, I felt empty. It wasn't until I started writing this book that I found my true purpose—to inspire, to connect, to help others through my words. Purpose didn't come from what I achieved—it came from what I gave.

2. A Story of Finding Direction

Let me tell you about my friend Priya, who discovered her purpose after years of feeling lost. Priya had a successful corporate job, but she felt unfulfilled. She'd go to work, come home, and feel like something was missing. She started volunteering at a local animal shelter on weekends, thinking it would just be a way to pass the time.

But at the shelter, Priya found her calling. She loved caring for the animals, helping them find homes, and educating people about animal welfare. She felt alive in a way she never had at her corporate job. Eventually, Priya left her career to start a nonprofit for animal rescue. She told me, "I thought purpose was about success, but it's about impact. This work gives my life meaning." Priya's story taught me that purpose often lies in what lights us up, in what we're willing to give our hearts to.

3. Why Purpose Matters

Purpose matters because it gives our lives meaning. It's the difference between surviving and thriving, between going through the motions and living fully. Purpose also gives us resilience—when we know why we're here, we can face any challenge, because we know it's part of a bigger picture.

I've seen this in my own life. Writing this book hasn't been easy—there have been days of doubt, days of exhaustion, days I wanted to give up. But my purpose—to inspire and help others—kept me going. Knowing that my words might make a difference gave me the strength to keep writing, even when it was hard.

4. Religious Teachings on Purpose

Spiritual traditions remind us that purpose is often tied to serving others, to aligning with a higher calling.

Bhagavad Gita:

"Your right is to work only, but never to its fruits."

— Chapter 2, Verse 47

The Gita teaches that purpose is about the work itself, not the outcome. When we focus on our duty, we find meaning.

Quran:

"I have only created jinn and men that they may serve Me."

— SurahAdh-Dhariyat 51:56

This verse reminds us that our ultimate purpose is to serve God, often through serving others. Purpose is a sacred calling.

5. Discovering Your Purpose

Purpose isn't something you find—it's something you uncover. It's often hidden in the things that light you up, the causes you care about, the ways you want to make a difference. To find your purpose, ask yourself: What makes me feel alive? What would I do even if I wasn't paid for it? How can I serve others?

I found my purpose through reflection. I asked myself what I loved, what I was good at, and what the world needed. Writing kept coming up—I loved it, I was good at it, and I believed it could help others. That clarity gave me direction, and it's guided me ever since.

6. A Purpose Practice

Here's a practice to help you uncover your purpose:

• Step 1: Write down three things you love to do—things that make you feel alive, that you'd do for free.

• Step 2: Write down three things you're good at—skills, talents, or qualities that come naturally to you.

• Step 3: Write down three ways you'd like to make a difference in the world. What causes matter to you?

• Step 4: Look for overlap between these lists. Where do your passions, skills, and desire to serve intersect? That's where your purpose lives. Reflect on how you can start living that purpose today.

I did this practice a few years ago, and it led me to writing. I loved storytelling, I was good at expressing emotions, and I wanted to inspire others. That intersection became my purpose, and it's shaped everything I've done since.

7. Purpose in the Everyday

Purpose doesn't have to be grand—it can be lived in the everyday. It's in the way you care for your family, the way you show up at work, the way you treat a stranger. Purpose isn't just about what you do—it's about how you do it.

Priya's story is a great example. Her purpose wasn't just about starting a nonprofit—it was about the love she brought to every animal she helped, every person she educated. Purpose isn't always big—it's often in the small, meaningful acts that make a difference.

8. The Compass That Never Fails

Purpose is the compass that guides your life. It keeps you on track, even when the road gets hard. It reminds you why you're here, what you're meant to do, who you're meant to be. I think back to Priya's story. Once she found her purpose, she never felt lost again. She had a direction, a calling, a reason to keep going.

I've felt this too. My purpose has guided me through every chapter of this book, through every doubt, through every challenge. Purpose doesn't just give you meaning—it gives you direction.

Final Words of This Chapter

Purpose is the compass that guides your life—find it, and you'll never feel lost. You don't have to have it all figured out—just start with what lights you up, what you're good at, what you want to give. Your purpose is waiting for you. What's one step you can take toward it today?

Chapter 55: The Strength of Gratitude

"Gratitude turns what you have into enough—it's the alchemy of the heart."

— Jagat Sandhu

1. The Magic of Gratitude

Gratitude is the practice of noticing and appreciating what's good in your life, no matter how small. It's the alchemy of the heart—turning what you have into enough, turning struggle into perspective, turning ordinary moments into miracles. Gratitude doesn't change your circumstances, but it changes how you see them, and that changes everything.

I've experienced the magic of gratitude firsthand. A few years ago, I was going through a tough time financially. I felt stressed, scared, and focused on everything I didn't have. But I started a gratitude practice—every night, I'd write down three things I was thankful for. Some days, it was as simple as "a warm bed, a good meal, a kind word from a friend." Slowly, my perspective shifted. I started to see how much I did have, how much I was blessed with. Gratitude didn't fix my finances, but it fixed my heart.

2. A Story of Perspective

Let me tell you about my cousin, Nisha, who found strength through gratitude. Nisha was diagnosed with a chronic illness that forced her to give up her career as a dancer—a career she loved. She felt angry, cheated, and focused on everything she'd lost. But one day, she started a gratitude journal. She'd write down small things she was thankful for—her family's support, the way the sun felt on her skin, the music she could still listen to.

Over time, gratitude changed Nisha's outlook. She started to see her illness not as a loss, but as a redirection. She began teaching dance to kids online, sharing her passion in a new way. Nisha told me, "Gratitude didn't take away my illness, but it gave me a reason to keep going. It showed me I still had so much to live for." Her story taught me that gratitude isn't about ignoring the hard stuff—it's about finding the good in the midst of it.

3. Why Gratitude Matters

Gratitude matters because it shifts your focus from lack to abundance, from despair to hope, from fear to love. Studies show that gratitude improves mental health, reduces stress, and even boosts physical well-being. But beyond the science, gratitude matters because it reminds us of life's goodness. It helps us see the blessings we might otherwise miss.

I've seen this in my own life. When I'm stressed, gratitude brings me back to center. I'll pause and think of something I'm thankful for—like the fact that I have a roof over my head, or the laughter of a loved one. That small act of gratitude changes my mood, my energy, my day. Gratitude isn't just a practice—it's a lifeline.

4. Religious Teachings on Thankfulness

Spiritual traditions emphasize gratitude as a sacred act, one that connects us to the divine and to each other.

Quran:

"If you are grateful, I will surely increase you in favor."

— Surah Ibrahim 14:7

This verse teaches that gratitude brings more blessings. When we appreciate what we have, we open the door for more.

Guru Granth Sahib Ji:

"Shukarkar, shukarkar, Nanak."

(Be grateful, be grateful, O Nanak.)

This teaching reminds us that gratitude is a way of life. It's a constant practice of giving thanks for the divine's gifts.

5. Gratitude in Hard Times

Gratitude isn't just for the good times—it's for the hard times too. When life feels heavy, gratitude can be a light. It doesn't mean you ignore your pain; it means you look for the small blessings that can help you through it.

Nisha's story is a perfect example. Her illness was devastating, but gratitude helped her find a new path. She didn't deny her pain—she just didn't let it define her. Gratitude gave her perspective, strength, and a way forward.

6. A Gratitude Practice

Here's a practice to help you cultivate gratitude:

• Step 1: Every morning, write down three things you're grateful for. Be specific—"I'm grateful for the way my coffee tasted today," or "I'm grateful for my friend's kind words."

• Step 2: Throughout the day, pause and notice something you're thankful for in the moment. It could be the warmth of the sun, a smile from a stranger, a quiet moment.

• Step 3: At the end of the day, share your gratitude with someone. Tell a loved one what you're thankful for, or post it online to spread the positivity.

• Step 4: Reflect on how gratitude changes your day. Do you feel lighter? More connected? More hopeful?

I've done this practice for years, and it's become a sacred part of my routine. This morning, I wrote: "I'm grateful for the sound of birds outside my window, the support of my readers, and the chance to write today." Gratitude sets the tone for my day—it reminds me to look for the good.

7. Gratitude as a Way of Life

Gratitude isn't just a practice—it's a way of life. It's about training your heart to see the good, even when it's hard to find. It's about saying thank you to the universe, to God, to the people around you, every single day.

I've seen this in Nisha's journey. Gratitude didn't just help her through her illness—it became her lens for living. She now starts every class she teaches with a moment of gratitude, asking her students to share something they're thankful for. Gratitude didn't just change her life—it changed the lives of those around her.

8. The Alchemy of Gratitude

Gratitude turns what you have into enough. It's the alchemy of the heart, transforming the ordinary into the extraordinary, the painful into the meaningful. I think back to my own financial struggles. Gratitude didn't change my bank account, but it changed my perspective. It reminded me that I had enough—enough love, enough strength, enough blessings—to keep going.

Final Words of This Chapter

Gratitude turns what you have into enough—it's the alchemy of the heart. You don't need more to be happy—you just need to see the beauty in what you already have. Start today, with a single thank you, and watch how it transforms your life. What are you grateful for right now?

Chapter 56: The Strength of Vulnerability

"Vulnerability is not weakness—it's the birthplace of connection, courage, and love."

— Jagat Sandhu

1. The Courage to Be Seen

Vulnerability is the act of showing up as you are—your fears, your flaws, your dreams, your truth. It's the courage to be seen, to let others in, to risk rejection for the sake of authenticity. We often think vulnerability is weakness, but it's the opposite—it's the birthplace of connection, courage, and love.

I used to be afraid of vulnerability. I'd hide my struggles, put on a brave face, pretend everything was fine. I thought that's what strength looked like. But I was wrong. It wasn't until I started sharing my true self—my doubts, my fears, my hopes—that I found real connection. Vulnerability didn't make me weak—it made me human.

2. A Story of Opening Up

Let me tell you about my friend Sameer, who discovered the power of vulnerability after years of hiding. Sameer was always the "strong one" in his family—he never cried, never showed fear, never admitted when he was struggling. But inside, he was battling anxiety. He felt overwhelmed but was too ashamed to tell anyone.

One day, Sameer broke down in front of his best friend. He shared everything—his anxiety, his fears, his exhaustion. He expected his friend to judge him, but instead, his friend hugged him and said, "I've been there too. You don't have to go through this alone." That moment of vulnerability opened the door to healing. Sameer started therapy, leaned on his loved ones, and found strength in being seen. He told me, "I thought vulnerability would make me weak, but it made me stronger than I've ever been." His story taught me that vulnerability isn't a risk—it's a gift.

3. Why Vulnerability Matters

Vulnerability matters because it's the foundation of connection. When you're vulnerable, you let others see the real you, and that creates space for real relationships. Vulnerability also builds courage—it takes bravery to show your true self, and that bravery spills over into other areas of your life. Most importantly, vulnerability allows you to love and be loved fully, without walls, without pretense.

I've seen this in my own life. When I started sharing my struggles with writing this book—my self-doubt, my fear of failure—my friends didn't judge me. They supported me, shared their own struggles, and we grew closer. Vulnerability didn't push them away—it pulled us together.

4. Religious Teachings on Humility

Spiritual traditions remind us that vulnerability is a form of humility, a way of surrendering our ego and connecting with others.

Bible:

"Blessed are the meek, for they will inherit the earth."

— Matthew 5:5

This verse teaches that humility and vulnerability are strengths, not weaknesses. When we're meek, we're open to divine blessings.

Guru Granth Sahib Ji:

"Nimratavichsewakarni."

(Serve with humility.)

This teaching reminds us that vulnerability—showing up humbly, as we are—allows us to serve and connect more deeply.

5. The Fear of Vulnerability

Vulnerability feels scary because it involves risk. What if we're rejected? What if we're judged? What if we're not enough? But the truth is, the right people will love you for your vulnerability, not in spite of it. And even if you're rejected, vulnerability is still worth it—it's better to be seen and rejected than to hide and never be loved for who you are.

I've felt this fear myself. When I first shared a rough draft of this book with a friend, I was terrified. What if she hated it? What if she thought I wasn't good enough? But I took the risk, and she loved it. Her support gave me the confidence to keep going. Vulnerability didn't break me—it built me.

6. A Vulnerability Practice

Here's a practice to help you embrace vulnerability:

• Step 1: Reflect on something you've been hiding—a struggle, a fear, a dream. Write it down.

- Step 2: Choose one person you trust—a friend, a family member, a partner. Share that piece of yourself with them. Be honest, be real.

- Step 3: Notice their response. Do they support you? Do they open up in return? How does it feel to be seen?

- Step 4: Reflect on the experience. How did vulnerability change your relationship, your sense of self, your courage?

I did this practice with my sister. I shared my fear that this book might not make a difference, that I might fail. She listened, hugged me, and said, "You've already made a difference to me." That moment of vulnerability deepened our bond and gave me the courage to keep writing.

7. Vulnerability as a Bridge

Vulnerability is a bridge—it connects us to others, to ourselves, to love. When we're vulnerable, we invite others to be vulnerable too, creating a cycle of authenticity and connection.

Sameer's story is a perfect example. His vulnerability didn't just help him—it helped his friend. After Sameer opened up, his friend shared his own struggles with anxiety, and they supported each other. Vulnerability didn't just heal Sameer—it built a stronger friendship.

8. The Strength in Being Seen

Vulnerability is not weakness—it's the birthplace of connection, courage, and love. It's the strength to say, "This is me, flaws and all," and to trust that you're enough. I think back to Sameer's story. Vulnerability didn't diminish him—it empowered him. It gave him the strength to face his anxiety, to seek help, to live more fully.

I've felt this strength too. Sharing my fears and dreams through this book has been one of the most vulnerable things I've ever done. But it's also been the most rewarding. Vulnerability has connected me to you, my reader, in a way I never thought possible.

Final Words of This Chapter

Vulnerability is not weakness—it's the birthplace of connection, courage, and love. Don't hide your true self—let it be seen, let it be loved. The world needs your authenticity, your heart, your story. Who can you be vulnerable with today?

Chapter 57: The Power of Simplicity

"Simplicity is the art of letting go of what doesn't matter to make room for what does."

— Jagat Sandhu

1. The Clutter of Modern Life

We live in a world that glorifies more—more stuff, more busyness, more noise. But more doesn't always mean better. Often, it just means clutter—physical clutter in our homes, mental clutter in our minds, emotional clutter in our hearts. Simplicity is the art of letting go of what doesn't matter to make room for what does. It's about focusing on the essentials, the things that bring you joy, peace, and meaning.

I've felt the weight of clutter myself. A few years ago, my life felt chaotic—my schedule was packed, my home was overflowing with stuff, my mind was racing with worries. I was so busy chasing more that I forgot what I was chasing. It wasn't until I embraced simplicity—decluttering my space, my time, my thoughts—that I found clarity and peace.

2. A Story of Less Is More

Let me tell you about my friend Rina, who discovered the power of simplicity after a period of overwhelm. Rina was a high-achieving lawyer, always working, always striving, always adding more to her plate. But she was burnt out—exhausted, irritable, and disconnected from her family. One day, she decided to simplify her life.

Rina started by decluttering her home—she donated clothes she didn't wear, gadgets she didn't use, items that just took up space.

Then she simplified her schedule—she cut back on unnecessary commitments, made time for rest, prioritized her family. Finally, she simplified her mind—she started meditating, letting go of perfectionism, focusing on what truly mattered. Rina told me, "I thought I needed more to be happy, but I needed less. Simplicity gave me back my life." Her story taught me that simplicity isn't about deprivation—it's about freedom.

3. Why Simplicity Matters

Simplicity matters because it creates space—space to breathe, to think, to live. When you let go of what doesn't matter, you make room for what does—your relationships, your passions, your peace. Simplicity also reduces stress. When your life is less cluttered, your mind is less cluttered, and you can focus on the present moment.

I've seen this in my own life. After decluttering my space and schedule, I felt lighter, more focused, more present. I had time to write, to connect with loved ones, to enjoy the small joys of life. Simplicity didn't take away from my life—it added to it.

4. Religious Teachings on Detachment

Spiritual traditions emphasize simplicity as a path to peace, often through detachment from material excess.

Bhagavad Gita:

"One who is unattached to the fruits of his work and who works as he is obligated is in the renounced order of life."

— Chapter 6, Verse 1

The Gita teaches that simplicity comes from letting go of attachment to material things and focusing on duty.

Bible:

"Do not store up for yourselves treasures on earth, where moths and vermin destroy."

— Matthew 6:19

This verse reminds us to focus on what lasts—love, faith, connection—not on temporary material things.

5. Simplifying Your Space

Simplicity starts with your environment. When your space is cluttered, it's hard to feel calm. Start small—choose one area, like a drawer or a closet, and declutter it. Ask yourself: Does this item bring me joy? Do I use it? If not, let it go.

I did this with my desk a few months ago. It was covered in papers, gadgets, random items I didn't need. I cleared it out, keeping only what I use for writing—a notebook, a pen, my laptop. Now, every time I sit down to write, I feel focused, calm, ready. Simplicity in my space created simplicity in my mind.

6. A Simplicity Practice

Here's a practice to help you embrace simplicity:

• Step 1: Choose one area of your life to simplify—your space, your schedule, or your thoughts.

• Step 2: Declutter that area. For your space, donate or discard items you don't need. For your schedule, say no to one unnecessary commitment. For your thoughts, write down worries and let them go.

• Step 3: Focus on what remains. What brings you joy, peace, or meaning? How can you give more energy to that?

• Step 4: Reflect on how simplicity feels. Do you feel lighter? More focused? More present?

I did this practice with my schedule. I realized I was overcommitted, saying yes to things that drained me. I canceled one event I didn't want to attend, and I used that time to rest. The relief I felt was immediate—simplicity gave me back my energy.

7. Simplicity in Relationships

Simplicity isn't just about stuff—it's about relationships too. Focus on the connections that matter, the ones that lift you up, the ones that feel mutual. Let go of relationships that drain you, that feel one-sided, that don't align with your values.

Rina's story is a great example. When she simplified her life, she also simplified her relationships. She stopped spending time with people who made her feel stressed and focused on her family, her true friends. Simplicity didn't isolate her—it connected her more deeply to the people who mattered.

8. The Freedom of Less

Simplicity is the art of letting go of what doesn't matter to make room for what does. It's the freedom to live with intention, to focus on what's essential, to create a life that feels light and meaningful. I think back to Rina's story. Simplicity didn't limit her—it liberated her. She found more joy, more peace, more connection in less.

I've felt this freedom too. Simplifying my life has given me the space to write, to love, to live fully. Simplicity isn't about having less—it's about having more of what matters.

Final Words of This Chapter

Simplicity is the art of letting go of what doesn't matter to make room for what does. You don't need more to be happy—you need less of what weighs you down. Simplify one thing today, and watch how it creates space for joy, peace, and meaning. What can you let go of right now?

Chapter 58: The Strength of Faith

"Faith is the bridge between where you are and where you're meant to be—walk it with courage."

— Jagat Sandhu

1. The Power of Belief

Faith is the belief in something greater—whether it's God, the universe, or the goodness of life. It's the trust that there's a bigger plan, even when you can't see it. Faith is the bridge between where you are and where you're meant to be, the light that guides you through uncertainty, the strength that keeps you going when the road feels hard.

I've leaned on faith many times in my life. When I started writing this book, I had no idea if it would succeed. I faced rejection, self-doubt, and countless obstacles. But my faith—in God, in my purpose, in the journey—kept me going. I trusted that if I kept showing up, the path would unfold. And it did.

2. A Story of Trust

Let me tell you about my friend Deepak, who found strength through faith during a dark time. Deepak lost his father unexpectedly, and the grief was overwhelming. He felt lost, angry, questioning why this had happened. He stopped praying, stopped believing, stopped hoping.

One day, Deepak visited a gurdwara, not because he wanted to, but because his mother asked him to. As he sat there, listening to the kirtan, something shifted. He felt a sense of peace, a whisper of faith returning. He started praying again, not for answers, but for strength. Over time, faith helped him heal. Deepak told me, "Faith didn't bring my father back, but it brought me back. It gave me a way to carry my grief." His story taught me that faith isn't about having all the answers—it's about trusting through the questions.

3. Why Faith Matters

Faith matters because it gives us hope, resilience, and peace. It reminds us that we're not alone, that there's a greater force at work, that our struggles have meaning. Faith also connects us to something bigger—it lifts us out of our small worries and into a larger perspective.

I've seen this in my own life. During a health scare a few years ago, I was terrified. But my faith gave me comfort—I prayed, I trusted, I believed that whatever happened, I'd be okay. That faith didn't take away my fear, but it gave me the strength to face it.

4. Religious Teachings on Faith

Spiritual traditions emphasize faith as a cornerstone of a meaningful life.

Quran:

"And whoever believes in Allah—He will guide his heart."

— SurahAt-Taghabun 64:11

This verse teaches that faith leads to guidance. When we trust in God, we find the path.

Guru Granth Sahib Ji:

"Jin premkio, tin hi prabhpaaio."

(Those who love, they alone find God.)

This teaching reminds us that faith, rooted in love, connects us to the divine.

5. Faith Through Uncertainty

Faith shines brightest in uncertainty. When we don't know what's next, faith gives us the courage to keep going. It's the belief that even in the unknown, there's a purpose, a plan, a light.

Deepak's story is a perfect example. He didn't know how to move forward after his father's death, but faith gave him a bridge. It didn't answer his questions, but it gave him the strength to live with them. Faith didn't erase his grief—it transformed it.

6. A Faith Practice

Here's a practice to help you strengthen your faith:

• Step 1: Reflect on a challenge you're facing. Write down your fears, your doubts, your hopes.

• Step 2: Spend a few minutes in prayer, meditation, or reflection. Connect with your higher power—whether it's God, the universe, or your inner wisdom.

• Step 3: Surrender your challenge to that higher power. Say, "I trust you to guide me. I'll do my part and let you do yours."

• Step 4: Reflect on how faith feels. Do you feel lighter? More hopeful? More supported?

I did this practice during a period of writer's block. I was frustrated, doubting my ability to finish this book. I prayed, asking for guidance, and surrendered my fears. The next day, the words started flowing again. Faith didn't just comfort me—it inspired me.

7. Faith in Action

Faith isn't just a feeling—it's an action. It's showing up, even when you're unsure. It's taking the next step, even when you can't see the whole path. It's trusting that the journey has meaning, even when it's hard.

I've seen this in my own journey. Writing this book required faith every day—faith in my purpose, faith in my words, faith in the process. That faith kept me going, even when I wanted to give up. Faith isn't passive—it's a powerful force that moves you forward.

8. The Bridge to Your Destiny

Faith is the bridge between where you are and where you're meant to be. It's the trust that everything—your struggles, your joys, your journey—is leading you somewhere beautiful. I think back to Deepak's story. Faith didn't just help him through his grief—it led him to a deeper connection with his family, with his spirituality, with himself.

I've felt this too. My faith has guided me through every page of this book, through every challenge, through every moment of doubt. Faith hasn't just been my bridge—it's been my wings.

Final Words of This Chapter

Faith is the bridge between where you are and where you're meant to be—walk it with courage. Trust the journey, trust the plan, trust the light. Even when you can't see the way, faith will guide you. What can you surrender to faith today?

Chapter 59: The Strength of Love

"Love is the greatest force in the universe—it heals, it transforms, it connects us all."

— Jagat Sandhu

1. The Universal Language of Love

Love is the greatest force in the universe. It's the energy that heals wounds, transforms hearts, and connects us all. Love isn't just romantic—it's the kindness you show a stranger, the compassion you give a friend, the care you give yourself. Love is the thread that weaves us together, the light that guides us home.

I've felt the power of love in my own life. After my breakup, I thought I'd never open my heart again. I was hurt, guarded, afraid. But my family's love—their patience, their support, their unwavering belief in me—helped me heal. Love didn't just mend my heart—it made it stronger.

2. A Story of Unconditional Love

Let me tell you about my friend Anjali, who showed me the transformative power of love. Anjali's teenage son, Rohan, started struggling with addiction. He'd lash out, lie, push her away. Anjali was heartbroken, but she refused to give up on him. She loved him unconditionally—she'd sit with him through his anger, drive him to rehab, pray for him every night.

Over time, Rohan started to change. He saw how much his mother loved him, how much she believed in him, even when he didn't believe in himself. That love gave him the strength to fight for his recovery. He's been sober for three years now, and he told me, "My mom's love saved my life. It showed me I was worth saving." Anjali's story taught me that love isn't just a feeling—it's a force, a choice, a lifeline.

3. Why Love Matters

Love matters because it's the essence of life. It's what makes us human, what gives us meaning, what keeps us going. Love heals— it mends broken hearts, soothes pain, restores hope. Love also connects us—it breaks down walls, builds bridges, reminds us that we're all one.

I've seen this in my own life. When I lost my friend to illness, I felt so much pain, but love got me through. The love of my family, the love of my community, the love I still felt for my friend—it all held me together. Love didn't take away my grief, but it gave me a way to carry it.

4. Religious Teachings on Love

Spiritual traditions remind us that love is divine, the highest expression of our humanity.

Bible:

"Love is patient, love is kind."

— 1 Corinthians 13:4

This verse teaches that love is a way of being—patient, kind, selfless. It's how we reflect God's love in the world.

Guru Granth Sahib Ji:

"Prempiaalaajopilaavai, so sant koi."

(One who offers the cup of love, that one is a true saint.)

This teaching reminds us that love is sacred. When we love, we embody the divine.

5. Loving Through the Hard Times

Love isn't always easy—it's often tested by pain, conflict, and struggle. But that's when love matters most. Loving through the hard times means showing up, even when it's messy, even when it hurts, even when you don't know how.

Anjali's story is a perfect example. Loving Rohan through his addiction wasn't easy—it was painful, exhausting, uncertain. But her love never wavered, and that steadfastness changed everything. Love isn't just for the good times—it's for the hard times too.

6. A Love Practice

Here's a practice to help you cultivate love in your life:

• Step 1: Reflect on someone you love—someone you're grateful for. Write down what you love about them.

• Step 2: Do something to show that love today. It could be a kind word, a thoughtful gesture, a moment of presence.

• Step 3: Extend that love to yourself. Write down three things you love about yourself, and treat yourself with the same kindness.

• Step 4: Reflect on how love feels. How does it change your day, your relationships, your heart?

I did this practice with my mom. I wrote down how much I love her strength, her humor, her warmth. I called her to tell her, and we ended up talking for an hour, laughing and sharing stories.

Then I wrote down things I love about myself—my creativity, my resilience, my heart. Love didn't just connect me to my mom—it connected me to myself.

7. Love as a Ripple Effect

Love has a ripple effect—what you give comes back, and it spreads to others. When you love someone, you inspire them to love, and that love touches everyone around them.

I've seen this with Anjali and Rohan. Anjali's love didn't just save Rohan—it inspired him to give back. He now volunteers at a rehab center, helping others through their struggles. Anjali's love created a chain reaction of healing and hope.

8. The Greatest Force

Love is the greatest force in the universe—it heals, it transforms, it connects us all. It's the answer to every question, the solution to every problem, the light in every darkness. I think back to Anjali's story. Her love didn't just change Rohan's life—it changed hers, and it changed everyone who witnessed it.

I've felt this force too. Love has carried me through every challenge, every heartbreak, every moment of doubt. It's the reason I wrote this book—to share love with you, to remind you that you're never alone.

Final Words of This Chapter

Love is the greatest force in the universe—it heals, it transforms, it connects us all. Choose love today—in your words, your actions, your heart. Let it guide you, let it heal you, let it connect you. Who can you show love to right now?

Chapter 60: The Journey Forward

"The journey isn't about reaching the end—it's about becoming who you're meant to be along the way."

— Jagat Sandhu

1. The Beauty of the Journey

Life is a journey, not a destination. We often focus on the end—on achieving our goals, on arriving at some perfect place—but the real beauty is in the journey itself. It's in the lessons we learn, the people we meet, the person we become along the way. The journey isn't about reaching the end—it's about becoming who you're meant to be.

Writing this book has been a journey for me. When I started, I thought it was about the finished product—a book I could hold in my hands, a dream I could check off my list. But along the way, I realized it was about so much more. It was about discovering my purpose, facing my fears, growing into the person I'm meant to be. The journey changed me, and that's the real gift.

2. A Story of Becoming

Let me tell you about my friend Kiran, who embodies the beauty of the journey. Kiran always dreamed of becoming a doctor, but her path was far from easy. She failed her entrance exams twice, faced financial struggles, and dealt with self-doubt. But she kept going, step by step, year by year.

After a decade of hard work, Kiran finally became a doctor. But when I asked her about her journey, she didn't talk about the degree—she talked about who she became along the way. She said,

"The journey taught me resilience, compassion, faith. I became a better person, not just a doctor." Kiran's story taught me that the journey isn't just about what you achieve—it's about who you become.

3. Why the Journey Matters

The journey matters because it's where growth happens. Every challenge, every joy, every moment shapes you, teaches you, prepares you for what's next. The journey also reminds us to stay present—to savor the process, to appreciate the now, to trust that everything is unfolding as it should.

I've seen this in my own life. Writing this book wasn't just about the end goal—it was about the daily act of showing up, the lessons I learned, the connections I made. Each chapter, each struggle, each breakthrough made me more of who I'm meant to be.

4. Religious Teachings on the Path

Spiritual traditions remind us that the journey is sacred, a path to self-discovery and divine connection.

Bhagavad Gita:

"The path of the righteous is beset with obstacles, but they reach their goal."

— Chapter 6, Verse 40

The Gita teaches that the journey, with all its challenges, leads us to our purpose.

Quran:

"Indeed, the straight path leads to Allah."

— SurahAl-Fatihah 1:6

This verse reminds us that the journey is a path to God. Every step, every moment, is sacred.

5. Embracing the Unknown

The journey often involves the unknown—twists, turns, detours we didn't expect. But that's where the magic happens. Embracing the unknown means trusting that every step, even the hard ones, is leading you somewhere beautiful.

Kiran's story is a perfect example. She didn't know if she'd ever become a doctor, but she kept walking her path, trusting the journey. The unknown didn't stop her—it shaped her. It made her who she is today.

6. A Journey Practice

Here's a practice to help you embrace your journey:

•   Step 1: Reflect on your journey so far. Write down three challenges you've faced and what they taught you.

• Step 2: Write down three joys you've experienced and how they shaped you.

• Step 3: Look ahead—what's one step you can take today to keep moving forward on your journey?

•   Step 4: Reflect on who you're becoming. How has the journey changed you? Who are you meant to be?

I did this practice recently. I reflected on the challenges of writing this book—self-doubt, rejection, time constraints—and realized they taught me resilience, patience, and trust. I thought about the joys—connecting with readers, finding my voice, finishing a chapter—and how they gave me confidence, purpose, and gratitude. The journey hasn't just been about the book—it's been about becoming a better version of myself.

7. The Journey as a Teacher

The journey is your greatest teacher. It shows you who you are, what you're capable of, what matters most. Every step—whether it's a stumble or a stride—is a lesson, a gift, a chance to grow.

I've learned so much from my journey. Writing this book taught me to trust myself, to be vulnerable, to keep going even when it's hard. The journey didn't just give me a book—it gave me a new understanding of myself, of life, of what I'm here to do.

8. Becoming Who You're Meant to Be

The journey isn't about reaching the end—it's about becoming who you're meant to be along the way. It's about growing into your purpose, your strength, your light. I think back to Kiran's story. Her journey didn't just make her a doctor—it made her a compassionate, resilient, faithful person. The journey was her true destination.

I've felt this too. This book has been a journey of becoming—of stepping into my purpose, of finding my voice, of connecting with you. The journey isn't over, and that's the beauty of it. There's always more to learn, more to grow, more to become.

Final Words of This Chapter

The journey isn't about reaching the end—it's about becoming who you're meant to be along the way. Embrace every step, every lesson, every moment. You're not just going somewhere—you're becoming someone. What has your journey taught you, and where will it take you next?

Acknowledgments

As I write the final words of Half Me, Half the World, I am filled with deep gratitude for those who have helped shape this book and my journey. This book is not only the result of my own thoughts and reflections but also the support, love, and encouragement I received from the amazing people around me.

A Special thanks To my sister, Akashdeep, thank you for being my constant pillar of support. Your encouragement, faith in me, and timely reminders to keep pushing forward were the fuel that kept me going during moments of doubt. Your belief in me has made all the difference.

To my mother, Mandeep Kaur, who taught me the values of hard work, perseverance, and kindness. Your wisdom has been the foundation of my life, and your unconditional love continues to inspire me every day. I am forever grateful for the lessons you've imparted to me.

And to my father, Lakhwinder Singh, thank you for your unwavering belief in me and for always being there with your strength and support. Your encouragement has been a guiding force in this journey, and I could not have done it without you.

To my beloved grandfather, Nirvail Singh, and grandmother, Gurjeet Kaur, your love, wisdom, and teachings continue to guide me. The lessons you have imparted to me are forever in my heart, and I carry your spirit and guidance with me as I continue to grow and learn.

 to my dear friend, Ravleen and Bharti, whose unwavering support and dedication played a crucial role in bringing this book to life. Your guidance, creativity, and ideas have been invaluable in shaping this work, and I cannot express enough how much your help has meant to me.

Lastly, to all the readers who have opened their hearts to the ideas and stories in these pages—thank you. This book is for you, and I hope that it inspires you to find balance, purpose, and meaning in your own life.

With deep gratitude and love,

Jagat Sandhu